Scheduling

the

Secondary School

Richard A. Dempsey
Henry P. Traverso

National Association of Secondary School Principals
1904 Association Drive, Reston, Virginia 22091

National Association of Secondary School Principals
1904 Association Drive, Reston, Virginia 22091

Contents

Figures

Foreword

School scheduling is hardly an esoteric science, but its procedures and techniques are less widely understood than might be assumed.

Knowledge of scheduling is one of the most important educational tools at the service of administrators, teachers, and students. The school schedule makes visible and evident the educational philosophy of the institution. If the philosophy is traditional, the schedule will likely be a conventional one. If the philosophy is nontraditional, the schedule will probably be flexible or individualized.

In either case, the quality of the schedule mirrors the competence and experience of the principal and the administrative team. Whether the schedule is conventional or flexible, it must provide appropriate course offerings, time arrangements suitable to effective instruction, and sufficient flexibility to support the individual learning needs of the students.

Scheduling techniques have changed frequently and dramatically since the early 1960s, in keeping with changing national priorities. The increase in school enrollments and proliferation of curricular offerings in the 1960s spurred the development of computerized scheduling techniques. The number of courses offered, the concern for equal opportunity, and the individualization of instruction resulted in a surge in the variety and flexibility of scheduling models available to schools. Expressions such as "SSSS," "GASP," "flex-mod," "block," and "arena" entered the educational lexicon. By the early 1970s, a growing awareness of accountability and the quality of individual opportunity prompted educators to revitalize conventional scheduling, and to take a fresh look at the options.

The school scheduler today must have a sophisticated knowledge of manual and computerized scheduling techniques, and a sensitivity to the delicate balance between flexibility and accountability in any truly effective schedule. A schedule can vary significantly from school to school and, with time, even in the same school. Some scheduling procedures are the same whether systems are manual or computerized, whether conventional or flexible techniques are employed. But each approach has its peculiarities. The effective administrator must be a master of these similarities and differences.

1

Richard Dempsey and Henry Traverso present here an excellent "how to do it" manual on the intricacies of school scheduling. Aspiring school administrators and first-time schedulers will find in this volume a wealth of technical information and common sense about the scheduling process. Experienced assistant principals, principals, and superintendents will value it as a staff development tool. University professors of school administration will appreciate its value for courses in school management.

The authors tell us that school scheduling is "a program and time design bringing students, teachers, curriculum, materials, and space into a systematic arrangement for the purpose of creating an optimal learning climate." The goal of the schedule, then, is to facilitate the functioning of the entire school program. Scheduling seeks to provide teachers and students with the freedom and structure to pursue worthwhile instructional goals. As such, it is perhaps the most significant basic skill of the effective school administrator.

The NASSP would like to recognize the national standing Committee of Professors of Secondary School Administration and Supervision (PSSAS) for suggesting and supporting the preparation of this important publication.

James W. Keefe
Director of Research
NASSP

Chapter One
Scheduling: An Overview

Effective scheduling of the secondary school is considered by many educators to be the supreme test of the administrator's management skills. The schedule reflects the principal's organizational ability; talent for carrying out precise planning; and awareness and concern for the needs of students, teachers, and the community. On the one hand, the schedule may effectively mirror good curriculum modeling and the consensual goals and objectives of the school and community. On the other hand, it may exhibit a bias toward specific groups and programs as well as the district's idiosyncratic interpretation of educational priorities.

Different names have been applied to this basic task of school administration in different parts of the United States. Some refer to the scheduling process as "rostering" or "registering"; others call it "blocking" or "pontooning." Most Canadian administrators describe it as "timetabling." The literature on the topic uniformly refers to "scheduling." We shall use the latter term.

Scheduling is a program and time design bringing students, teachers, curriculum, materials, and space into a systematic arrangement for the purpose of creating an optimal learning climate. When carefully done, scheduling facilitates the curricular and personnel decisions of the entire school community.

Though considered by most practitioners to be complex and perhaps the most fundamental task associated with an effective school, scheduling does not receive the same attention from every principal. Some embrace it as their unquestioned professional responsibility; others delegate it to staff members. Whatever the administrative arrangement, no principal should be far removed from the schedule planning process.

RESPONSIBILITIES FOR SCHEDULING

Responsibility of the School Community

In a school characterized by the regular movement of students from one learning station to another, scheduling is the facilitator of the learning process, the overriding medium through which instructional goals are achieved. Everyone within the school community plays a part: the principal and the administrative team; the faculty—department heads, teachers, and counselors; the students, whose role can be made as active as the other participants; the members of the board of education; the parents; the superintendent of schools; and other central office personnel who can enhance or exacerbate the scheduling process.

The schedule is such an essential component of the school program that no school can function effectively without a good one. Ideas become reality through scheduling; courses become classes; programs of instruction are transformed into student schedules; mornings and afternoons become instructional periods or modules; goals become events. Through scheduling, the school mingles all of its essential facets—faculty and staff, curriculum, space and facilities, students—into an integrated and efficient learning environment.

Responsibility of the Principal

No "law" demands that the building principal be the scheduling administrator. Since the principal is the educational leader of the building, however, it is clearly his or her responsibility to organize and oversee the entire scheduling process. Many of the specific scheduling duties may be delegated appropriately to assistant principals, department heads, and counselors, but the principal must direct and supervise the procedures to be followed. Decisions about the basic structure of the schedule, lengths of courses, number of minutes per course days in the cycle, number of periods per day, etc., should reflect the principal's leadership and guidance. All school persons who are affected should have a voice in these important matters, but only the principal can provide the focus and direction.

PURPOSES OF SCHEDULING

Scheduling and the Curriculum

The curriculum is only words on paper or in the minds of people until it is actualized through the scheduling process. Whatever its source—guides published by the state, county, or individual districts; manuscripts written by teams of teachers during lengthy periods of time; or materials purchased from commercial outlets—the secondary curriculum requires a systematic vehicle for implementation. This medium is the scheduling process or, more specifically, the *master schedule*.

Curriculum goals and objectives become specific courses in the master schedule. Through scheduling, these courses bring together students, teachers, activities, and facilities so that the instructional goals can be implemented.

Scheduling and the Student

Students are the real reason for the schedule. Scheduling directly serves the needs of students by providing them with personal learning opportunities. Students can also participate actively in this process. In "student self-scheduling," for example, students help determine their individual schedules. This is in contrast to totally computerized scheduling, where students receive a schedule that has largely been organized by others. The degree to which students are allowed to contribute to the scheduling process reflects the school's educational philosophy, the flexibility of its scheduling mechanisms, administrative awareness of options, and the willingness of the school to promote student participation.

Scheduling and the Faculty

The outcomes of scheduling have a direct impact on the faculty; indeed, the schedule affects the manner in which faculty members function throughout the year. For example, if long-standing, effective working relationships are disrupted, if teachers are required to teach subjects for which they are inadequately prepared, if teachers must travel to several different classrooms to carry out their assignments, their teaching may be impaired.

Teachers are matched with courses and students in a particular facility at a specified time of day. Depending on school policies, however, teachers may play either an extensive or a limited role in the scheduling process. They may be called upon to serve as resource persons for the courses within their own departments; their advice may be sought about a particular student enrolling in an elective course. In some schools, the faculty's role in scheduling has been expanded to decisions regarding course offerings, length of courses, approval of students in specific courses, membership on the school's "scheduling committee," construction of the master schedule, and—in the event of student self-scheduling—the handling of certain duties at the scheduling site (usually called the "arena").

SCHOOL EDUCATIONAL PHILOSOPHY

Since schools should act according to their institutional beliefs, the relationship between the established educational philosophy of the school and the scheduling process should be direct and harmonious. School-adopted guidelines for student scheduling represent a particular philosophical position. If these guidelines are in concert with the fundamental purposes of the school and district, the schedule should be sound. Should the guidelines and the beliefs not be in accord, the scheduling process may serve to establish an environment that is counterproductive to learning.

The scheduling cycle includes a significant number of steps. Each of these steps must be developed with a common point of reference—the educational philosophy of the school.

STATE AND LOCAL REQUIREMENTS

State and/or local requirements may affect the way in which a schedule is built. The secondary school administrator should be aware of these external requirements and any restrictions they might impose.

Generally, state departments of education mandate specific curricular areas to be offered, such as English, mathematics, science, and the arts. Curriculum guides and approved texts may be identified as well as instruments for evaluating student attainment of instructional goals. Some states allow schools little or no deviation from prescribed programs; others permit great flexibility under very general guidelines.

At the local level, board of education policies can be narrowly prescriptive or sufficiently broad to allow for building-level decision making. Even though the curriculum may be totally determined and rigidly monitored by the school board or a committee, administrators still will probably determine the form and arrangement of the schedule. The administrator must differentiate between those aspects of scheduling which do or do not allow for local option.

CHOOSING A SCHEDULING SYSTEM

Within the past two decades, the number of scheduling system options has increased significantly. From a procedure that was manual from beginning to end, scheduling has progressed technically from keysort approaches to first-generation computers to present-day microcomputers. Scheduling may make limited use of the computer or may use service bureaus and time-sharing that offer highly sophisticated options.

Manual Scheduling

Schools that perform all scheduling operations manually usually have limited financial resources, small student enrollments, or narrow curricular requirements. Highly efficient master schedules can be built manually using a conflict matrix, a procedure that is explained in Chapter Five.

Once the master schedule has been constructed, individual student schedules can be produced by a variety of methods, most handed down through the years from scheduler to scheduler. Among these are key-sort devices, post office-type sorting bins, class packs or student packs built from preprinted forms, needle devices, and "dot" or "check" methods. A "manually-run" arena is used in many schools.

Computer Scheduling

Data processing hardware and software are now commonly used in the scheduling process. In some schools, computer assistance is limited to producing course tallies needed to establish staffing requirements, to produce a conflict matrix, or both. The master schedule is built manually, and student schedules are produced by hand or in a "manual arena."

The most widely used scheduling format is one in which the computer generates the data from which the master schedule is hand built. These data include course tallies and the conflict matrix. After the schedule is built, the computer tests the efficiency of the master schedule (through a "simulation" run), loads or places the students into the master schedule, and produces student schedules, class lists, and other helpful reports.

Schools with very complex schedules as well as those with direct access to a local computer utilize the computer much more extensively. In these schools, the computer builds the master schedule. The scheduler simply provides information on available courses, teachers, rooms, and any restrictive factors that must be taken into account.

An increasing number of software packages are available to perform this task. Many mini-computer and microcomputer firms claim the capability of performing the entire scheduling operation, along with payroll, budgeting, accounting, and other computer services. Though forms must be coded and data interpreted, completely computerized scheduling does eliminate many of the laborious procedures associated with manual approaches.

Chapter Two
Specific Considerations for Scheduling

THE SCHOOL SCHEDULER must be knowledgeable of district and school policies and procedures about such topics as graduation requirements, length of courses, periods in the school day, days in the scheduling cycle, building clusters, program modifications, study hall configurations, and lunch schedules.

Student Graduation and Course Load Requirements

Whether established by state, province, county, or the local school board, graduation requirements and student course load regulations are basic to the scheduling process. Students must earn the number of credits that are required both for promotion and for graduation, and schedule within the minimum and maximum number of subjects allowed in a given year. All school personnel who participate in the scheduling cycle—administrators, guidance counselors, department heads, and teachers—must monitor student schedules to ensure conformance with school policies. Schools with data processing equipment can easily use the computer program to identify students with insufficient credits and courses for graduation. Once data have been collected and organized, students and parents can be kept abreast of student progress.

Length of Courses

Both required and elective courses come in varying lengths. While most courses are full-year or half-year in duration, shorter "mini-courses" have been introduced in recent years. Some courses follow a trimester pattern of approximately 12 weeks; others are quarter-courses of about 9 weeks. Schools with very flexible patterns have introduced "micro-courses" that last from several days to several weeks.

What is important for the scheduler to realize is that the lengths of the various courses must be compatible. Full-year, half-year, and quarter courses are reconcilable within the same time structure, but trimester courses would conflict unless taken only by students in a particular grade or program. Freshmen and sophomores, for example, could combine year-long and trimester courses, while juniors and seniors might be scheduled for full-year, semester, or quarter courses. Even this arrangement can present a problem in smaller schools where students in different grades are permitted to take courses together (e.g., chorus, typing, art).

Periods per School Day

The range in number of periods per school day varies from as few as 4 to as many as 32. Since the number of hours in the school day is relatively constant from district to district, an increase or decrease in the number of periods results in a decrease or increase in the length of each period. The flexible modular schedule uses more 12-15 minute modules than the conventional 45-60 minute periods found in traditional schedules. These schedules are reviewed in more detail in Chapter Three.

Schedulers should note that any change in either the number of periods per day or the number of minutes per period will inversely affect the other component. As the number of periods increases, the minutes per period will decrease. In some Canadian schools, for instance, the school day has been reduced to four periods to permit a series of double-block combinations.

In an effort to provide meaningful extracurricular activities, some schools may add a period to the school day—an activity period. During this time, student-oriented social, athletic, recreational, and academic activities are offered. Special transportation is usually arranged for students who wish to participate.

Days in the Scheduling Cycle

In many parts of the United States and throughout much of Canada, the traditional Monday through Friday schedule, known as a five-day cycle, has been replaced by some interesting alternatives. The most popular variation is the six-day cycle initially associated with the flexible modular schedule. (A detailed explanation of this model appeared in the December 1980 *NASSP Bulletin.*)

Some of the advantages of the six-day cycle are:

- Since classes can meet each day, every third day, or every second day, each arrangement meshes smoothly.
- More opportunity is available to neutralize the effects of holidays and inclement weather on the number of course meetings.
- There is much greater scheduling flexibility.

Period or Program Modifications

In the contemporary high school, specialized courses require special scheduling arrangements. Laboratory courses in science, industrial arts, home economics, and certain vocational-technical subjects demand greater time allotments. Early release programs such as work-study, distributive education, and health occupations education require much greater accommodation within the master schedule than those programs which have all required courses in one half and special electives in the other half of the school day.

House Plans

In very large or structurally unique schools, the physical space and the students may be organized in a school-within-a-school, or "house plan" arrangement. Principals of schools with several thousand students may choose to divide the building into several "houses" to produce smaller administrative units, each with its own administrator (usually called a housemaster), faculty, and unique set of classrooms. School climate is improved when students are able to identify with a smaller unit of 800 to 1,200 youngsters, rather than with a group of 2,000 to 3,000. Computer scheduling facilitates the house-plan concept and allows the scheduler to structure either a completely self-contained unit (called a "strong house plan") or a partially self-contained unit (referred to as a "weak house plan.") The selection of these options depends on the number of gymnasiums, cafeterias, and specialized classrooms that are available.

Study Halls

It is generally a local decision whether to have supervised study halls for unscheduled student time or to allow them to use lounges or commons, or to leave the campus. Both philosophical considerations and space limitations play an important role in this determination. What must be considered within each school is the effect that class loading patterns have on the number of students who have unstructured time.

Again, an inverse relationship exists between the number of students assigned to classes in a given period and the number available for study hall or other assignments. The fewer students assigned to classrooms in a period, the greater the number who must be placed in other options. Effective scheduling procedures will ensure that a relatively equal number of students are assigned to classes each period of the day, and that a balanced number will be available for study halls or other areas.

Lunch Period Models

Fortunately, there are many ways to schedule a hungry student. The choice an administrator makes is dependent on several factors:

- The size of the student body;
- The seating capacity of the cafeteria;
- The number of instructional periods in the school day;
- The length of the academic periods;
- The length of the lunch periods.

Lunch can be scheduled during part of an extended instructional period, during a separate block of time while some classes are in session, or at a time when no classes are being held. Figures 1, 2, and 3 illustrate lunch period models in schools with one or more extended instructional periods.

Figure 1
Three-Wave Lunch Over One Period

Wave One	*Wave Two*	*Wave Three*
Lunch 11:00-11:30	Class 11:00-11:30	Class 11:00-12:00
Class 11:30-12:30	Lunch 11:30-12:00	Lunch 12:00-12:30
	Class 12:00-12:30	

Advantages: Simple to implement. Contains only one split section.

Disadvantages: Provides little time for cafeteria clean-up; can produce serious traffic flow problem; breaks up an instructional period for approximately one-third of the student body.

Figure 2
Three-Wave Lunch Over Two Periods

Wave One		*Wave Two*		*Wave Three*	
Lunch	11:12-11:42	Period 4	11:12-12:04	Period 4	11:12-12:04
Period 4	11:42-12:34	Lunch	12:04-12:34	Period 5	12:04-12:56
Period 5	12:23- 1:26	Period 5	12:34- 1:26	Lunch	12:56- 1:26

Advantages: No split class sections; cafeteria clean-up time is provided; little or no traffic flow problems.

Disadvantages: Scheduling of teachers for cafeteria supervision can be a problem; computer loading of students into study halls must be monitored closely.

Figure 3
Five-Wave Lunch Over Two Periods

First Wave	Lunch	11:40-12:10
	Class	12:10- 1:10
Second Wave	Class	11:40-11:55
	Lunch	11:55-12:25
	Class	12:25- 1:10
Third Wave	Class	11:40-12:10
	Lunch	12:10-12:40
	Class	12:40- 1:10
Fourth Wave	Class	11:40-12:45
	Lunch	12:25-12:55
	Class	12:55- 1:10
Fifth Wave	Class	11:40-12:40
	Lunch	12:40- 1:10

Advantages: Allows scheduling of large numbers of students into a small cafeteria.

Disadvantages: Three instructional periods are interrupted by split lunches; little or no opportunity for cafeteria clean-up; traffic flow must be closely monitored.

STAFFING REQUIREMENTS AND CONSIDERATIONS

A host of factors impinge on staffing requirements. Budgetary constraints, student enrollment, and restrictions imposed by the teacher union contract (where it exists) have the most definable effect. Most of the responsibility for integrating student course requests with available teacher time will rest with the scheduler. Indeed, even if staffing decisions are to be made at higher administrative levels, the scheduler must first gather and interpret the data upon which these judgments will rest.

Variable Staff Loads

Decisions about variable staff load reflect local conditions, and must be based on a sound educational rationale. The scheduler must consider the possible variations when projecting the number of teacher sections needed to accommodate student requests. Some staff assignments usually include reduced teaching loads: subject supervisors, department heads, teachers of laboratory-oriented courses, team-teaching pairs or groups, teachers associated with work-experience assignments, and coaches during the sports season. Obviously, as course loads are lowered for assignments such as these, additional staff members will be required to offer the same opportunities for students.

Implications of Course Tallies

Although student population figures give some estimate of staffing needs, course tallies obtained during the registration process provide the most useful indicator of specific subject area needs. The number of students in a school may remain reasonably constant from one year to the next, but student course electives may signal the need for fewer teachers in one department and additional teachers in another. Moreover, in an era of declining enrollments, schedulers are faced with the undesirable task of interpreting data with direct consequences for teacher layoffs. Schedulers can even be the recipients of teacher enmity, since most reduction-in-force decisions can ultimately be traced to the tallies and determinations of the scheduler.

Emotional considerations notwithstanding, scheduling decisions are subject to a simple mathematical equation:

The Number of Student Sections of Courses Offered $=$ The Number of Available Teacher Sections

As an illustration of this mathematical necessity, consider the following hypothetical registration data for a high school:

Department	Combined Course Tallies
English	500 students
Mathematics	375 students
Science	375 students
Social Studies	250 students

If each section of each course were to have 25 students, and each teacher were to be assigned five classes, the school would need the following plan:

Department	Tallies	Sections Needed	Teachers Needed
English	500	20 $(500 \div 25)$	4 $(20 \div 5)$
Mathematics	375	15 $(375 \div 25)$	3 $(15 \div 5)$
Science	375	15 $(375 \div 25)$	3 $(15 \div 5)$
Social Studies	250	10 $(250 \div 25)$	2 $(10 \div 5)$

A total of 12 teachers would be required, each teacher with five classes for a total of 60 sections. In this example, any change in the number of available teacher sections resulting from budgetary or any other constraints would necessitate a corresponding reduction in the number of student sections offered. This reduction could be offset only by increasing the average class size (more than 25) or the average teacher load (more than five classes).

Cocurricular Assignments

A wide variety of cocurricular assignments exist, as well as sharply differing remuneration practices. It is difficult to suggest any universal method for schedulers to follow in confronting this issue. The "Douglass Formula" (Douglass, 1963) sought to equate teaching assignments by considering a variety of factors, including cocurricular responsibilities. In the contemporary secondary school, however, the scheduler's main concern is whether certain kinds of student cocurricular activities are to be scheduled with regular classes. If they are, then these assignments should be treated in the same manner as courses. If only one period is designated for all activities, then tighter control of student preferences and selections will have to be exercised.

The scheduler, for example, can accommodate student sports activities. A teacher/coach might be assigned an end-of-day preparation and planning period to make sufficient time available to organize for and receive the team.

Team Teaching

The decision to organize a school, a department, or just several pairs of teachers into team teaching units is a local one. Many questions should be resolved prior to the initiation of this instructional model. From a scheduler's point of view, team teaching may cause some problems in the master schedule.

An immediate effect of teaming is the creation of large single-course sections. In certain settings such as middle schools or junior high schools where the pattern may be school-wide, no unusual constraints are caused, and students can be easily handled by the respective teams (i.e., 100 to 125 students with four teachers). But in a high school where two teachers in one department team with 40 to 50 students, the existence of a large, single section of students can easily increase the number of potential conflicts. Scheduling the members of a team with a common planning period is a useful way to increase the effectiveness of the team teaching strategy.

13

Long-Term Considerations

A school enrolling 1,200 or more students must be able to offer a varied curriculum to meet the academic and vocational needs of its students. The imperatives here, of course, are reasonable budgetary support and adequate enrollments. When enrollments decrease sharply, it becomes increasingly difficult to provide a comprehensive program. In times of retrenchment, many factors inhibit the scheduler's flexibility to build a master schedule that is relatively conflict-free, yet offers an adequate number of limited section courses.

School decision makers and schedulers periodically face a number of issues that affect schedule planning:

- An increase in the number of requested courses, but fewer sections (thus increasing the probability of scheduling conflicts);
- A reduction in available staff (with a consequent need for teachers with dual or multiple certification);
- An acute teacher shortage in certain areas (e.g., mathematics, science, and the vocational areas);
- Added pressure for more required courses (many of which run for the full year);
- Any general tightening-up process (resulting in a reduction of elective and mini-courses).

BUILDING LAYOUT

More than any other administrator, the scheduler must be thoroughly familiar with the school building. In putting together the master schedule, the scheduler must make the most efficient use of available space, differentiating among general purpose classrooms, specialized classrooms, large-group rooms, small-group rooms, seminar rooms, school-within-school, and departmental arrangements.

Knowledge of the basic floor plan of the school enables the scheduler to make such sound decisions as ensuring the even flow of student traffic throughout the building, especially to and from the cafeteria and the gymnasium, and in the stairwells.

If departments are assigned specific locations within the building the scheduler must allocate enough rooms for each department in the proper area, allowing for any interchange of rooms that may be necessary. The scheduler must also be aware of those teachers who operate without a homeroom station, or who work in more than one department.

Significant variances in the room size can create opportunities for the scheduler. Large rooms are especially suited for team-teaching stations, as sites for audiovisual presentations, and for study halls. For low-enrollment classes such as seminars and project-oriented courses, small-group rooms are appropriate and should be assigned to make maximum use of space.

New schedulers should be cautious when assigning specialized rooms. Some of these rooms are so subject or skill-specific that a misassignment can be dangerous, costly, or (at the least) embarrassing for the scheduler. Consider the problems of a chemistry lab assigned as a homeroom, or a

14

choral room assigned to a small group. The scheduler should double-check all assignments to rooms such as language labs, stenography labs, industrial arts areas, art and music rooms, home economics suites, typing and office machines, and science labs.

A well-designed room chart showing the dimensions and listing estimated capacity is a necessity for any well-organized scheduler. Such a chart will help prevent the improper placement of students and the inappropriate use of rooms.

THE CURRICULUM

The components that link students to the curriculum fall under the direct supervision of the scheduler. The scheduler should be an expert on the school curriculum, its policies and practices. The scheduler will be responsible for developing publications and forms that facilitate the registration and scheduling processes.

Program of Studies

The scheduler must be thoroughly familiar with and keep current the school's catalog of course offerings. The most helpful course catalogs list complete information about departmental offerings, required and elective courses, course descriptions, course credits, classification and weighting of courses (e.g., advanced placement), grouping patterns (homogeneous or heterogeneous), graduation and promotion requirements, concurrent vocational school offerings, and recommended curricula. A well-formulated and well-designed catalog helps both students and parents make appropriate decisions about programs and course selections.

Student Registration Process

With course catalogs in hand, students begin the course registration process, usually with the assistance of guidance counselors, teacher advisers, and others involved in advisement procedures. Registration data are collected on course registration sheets (for manual or computerized scheduling) or computer cards. Registration sheets or cards contain the name and a number of every course planned to be offered. They can be color-coded to represent a particular class or group (seventh grade, sophomores). In highly computerized systems, recent technological advances permit the entry of these data directly from a terminal located in the school.

From the scheduler's viewpoint, accuracy of registration data is of paramount importance. One method of ensuring accuracy with data processing equipment is to print a "Course Verification Report." This inexpensive and simple form is sent to parents for verification. In this way, parents can detect any unauthorized changes in the student's schedule and identify any errors made during the processing of the data.

Once the registration data are verified, they are tallied by hand or machine to produce the course registration tallies. At this point, decisions can be made about which courses to drop because of insufficient enrollment, which courses to be merged because of low enrollments, the number of sections to be offered in each course, what the teaching staff size should be, etc.

Preregistration Form

Increasingly, schedulers are finding it useful to identify certain courses which need early monitoring to avoid overloading during the regular registration period. Preregistration makes advance planning possible for highly specialized courses that otherwise would be oversubscribed. Schedulers can control the numbers of registrations in these courses by limiting enrollment to certain classes (e.g., juniors or seniors). In offerings such as advanced levels of foreign languages, schedulers will know ahead of time that certain courses cannot be offered because of insufficient interest. Arrangements can be made to merge classes or to establish independent study opportunities. Obviously, experience is the best instructor for utilizing the pre-registration period data. Problem courses vary from school to school, as do building limitations and simple differences in student and parent preferences.

SCHEDULING RESTRICTIONS

An awareness of any predictable restrictions to the scheduling process will allow the scheduler to plan strategies accordingly. Certain restrictive factors must be addressed early in the process to avoid complications when the cycle is well underway. An axiom of scheduling is that the more extensive the restrictions, the more complex the scheduling.

Staff

Examples of staffing restrictions are teachers who work only part-time in a particular building (itinerant faculty), limited staff available to teach specialized courses, faculty members with reduced teaching assignments such as department heads or subject area supervisors, and those assigned to team teach. Teachers who supervise work-experience students also impose restrictions on the scheduler's flexibility, since these teachers must periodically be absent from the building to travel to the work sites.

Rooms

Some classrooms serve only specific purposes: language labs, science labs, typing rooms, physical education facilities, music and art rooms, and shops. Multi-purpose classrooms may have seating restrictions. A precise accounting of these rooms is essential for successful scheduling.

Courses

Those courses which involve unusual scheduling requirements should be identified before the process begins. Combination science/laboratory courses, vocational courses such as distributive education, mini-courses, team-taught courses, and other such variations all demand special attention and must be carefully placed in the master schedule.

Negotiated Contracts

Any teacher assignment requirements that are established by contracts negotiated with teacher unions tend to restrict the scheduler's flexibility. Some of the most common contractual items are class size, number of courses assigned per teacher, number of distinct preparations per teacher, and number of consecutive teaching periods. While these goals may be desirable from an educational point of view, their implementation can create problems for the scheduling process. For this reason, contract language which reads, "Every best effort will be made to . . . " is preferable to mandates. Obviously, a good faith effort is important to effective scheduling.

Chapter Three
The Scheduling Models

A WIDE DIVERSITY of educational thought becomes evident when one examines the scheduling models in use throughout North America. Not only are there a myriad of themes, but there are also variations on those themes. School principals apparently continue to search for the elusive "perfect" schedule.

Two popular types of schedule are near opposite ends of the scheduling continuum. They are the conventional or traditional model illustrated in Figure 1, and the flexible modular schedule depicted in Figure 2. Many other models exist, developed usually to meet specific educational needs or to make objective some philosophical perspective of the curriculum.

Conventional and Flexible

The basic traditional schedule (Figure 1) remains popular, and is used in the majority of secondary schools. Many schedulers return to the security of the traditional model after experimenting with other models because of its simplicity and noncontroversial character.

Characteristics of the conventional scheduling model are:

1. Classes meet the same time every day throughout the week. Exceptions are courses such as labs or physical education which may meet fewer than five times a week.
2. Every week is the same for teachers and students.
3. All periods are equal in length, requiring teachers to adopt instructional strategies that are workable within a fixed time slot.
4. Combining several same-subject classes into a large group is more difficult because related classes do not necessarily coincide.
5. Work experience programs can easily be scheduled, as well as morning and afternoon sessions at cooperating vocational-technical schools.
6. If lunch is served during one or two of the instructional periods, student traffic is simple to manage and is relatively constant from day to day.
7. Part-time faculty and specialized teaching assignments can readily be accommodated.

Figure 1
Traditional Schedule

	Monday	Tuesday	Wednesday	Thursday	Friday
1	A	A	A	A	A
2	B	B	B	B	B
3	C	C	C	C	C
4	D	D	D	D	D
5	E	E	E	E	E
6	F	F	F	F	F
7	G	G	G	G	G

Computerized scheduling technology has caused some break during the past two decades in the hold of traditional scheduling practices on middle level and senior high schools. With the assistance of funding from private foundations and the federal government, and consultative help from universities, many schools have initiated projects designed to reformulate the school schedule in more student-centered ways. Concepts such as large-group instruction, small-group learning, independent study experiences, and departmental resource centers have been developed.

The flexible modular (flex-mod) schedule is one of the most notable examples of this newer generation of scheduling models (Figure 2). This schedule has a number of prominent features:

1. The variety of choices in time pattern appears to be unlimited. Within the same subject area, courses can be scheduled to meet in as many different ways as the imagination allows.
2. Large numbers of students can be scheduled together in one location (e.g., an auditorium) for a lecture, a film, or some similar presentation.
3. The same group of students can be subdivided into smaller units for shorter frames on other days. Small-group discussions, simulations, student projects, and other activities can take place to reinforce the lessons of the large-group activity.
4. In psychomotor skill development areas such as typing, a flex-mod schedule can provide a conventional instructional period of 45 to 60 minutes per day for each day of a cycle.

5. Certain subjects such as art, music, physical education, consumer education/home economics, industrial arts, and lab sciences can be scheduled into 75 to 90-minute blocks, meeting on alternate days of a cycle, if desired.
6. Some "unscheduled time" results in the flex-mod schedule, calling for careful choices on the part of students, parents, and academic advisers.

Schools that have successfully incorporated the concepts of flex-mod scheduling usually reflect a number of similar characteristics. Some of the essential ingredients are the following:

1. Strong administrative leadership to ensure proper implementation of the model. The principal is the key to the program's success.
2. Thorough planning, involving administrators, teachers, counselors, parents, school board members, and students. A minimum of two years of preparation is usually necessary.
3. Selective implementation based on departmental needs. Some departments may wish to operate within a conventional framework.
4. Flexible physical space to accommodate small, medium, and large-group instruction, team teaching, departmental resource centers, central learning stations, and independent study experiences.
5. Advisement for students to make good decisions about the use of instructional time. Some students may require close monitoring since large amounts of unscheduled time can be a by-product of the process.
6. Continued support of the board of education, parents, and the community. Scheduling innovations frequently generate community antipathy as problems surface.

Modular

Administrators who wish to gain the advantages of a more flexible schedule without its problems have restructured their conventional schedules to provide time variations. Figure 3 illustrates a typical student schedule in a 15-module framework. Each module is 25 minutes long. Certain subjects such as Algebra I are offered in conventional 50-minute classes each day of the five-day cycle. However, physical education and science labs are scheduled for 75-minute uninterrupted blocks. Within this conventional modular schedule, team teaching and some large-group activities can exist.

Other creative schedulers have devised similar modular patterns to provide time variations. Mods number from 10 to 20, and are 15-30 minutes in length.

Static and Rotating

There are critics of the flex-mod schedule who argue that, once in place, even with its many possibilities, the flex-mod is a very static schedule. School districts with ready access to a computer and a data processing staff adjust the basic flex-mod schedule periodically to meet changing curricular objectives. Some districts, for example, construct a new schedule every nine

Figure 2
Student Flexible Modular Schedule; Six-Day Cycle

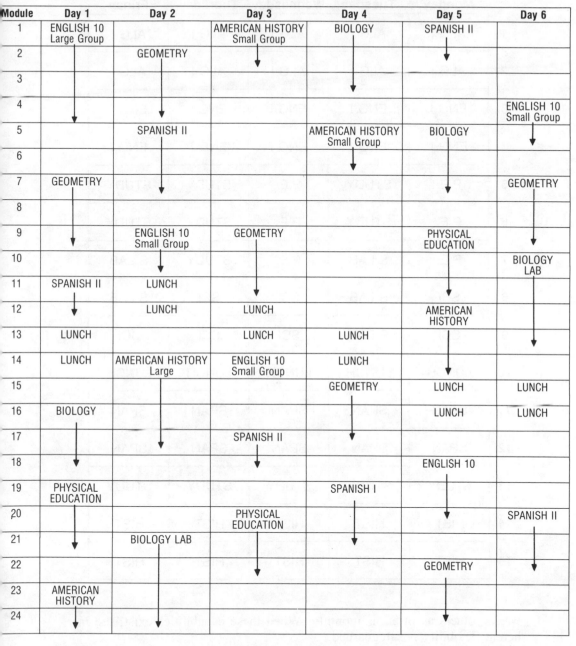

Module	Day 1	Day 2	Day 3	Day 4	Day 5	Day 6
1	ENGLISH 10 Large Group		AMERICAN HISTORY Small Group	BIOLOGY	SPANISH II	
2		GEOMETRY				
3						
4						ENGLISH 10 Small Group
5		SPANISH II		AMERICAN HISTORY Small Group	BIOLOGY	
6						
7	GEOMETRY					GEOMETRY
8						
9		ENGLISH 10 Small Group	GEOMETRY		PHYSICAL EDUCATION	
10						BIOLOGY LAB
11	SPANISH II	LUNCH				
12		LUNCH	LUNCH		AMERICAN HISTORY	
13	LUNCH		LUNCH	LUNCH		
14	LUNCH	AMERICAN HISTORY Large	ENGLISH 10 Small Group	LUNCH		
15				GEOMETRY	LUNCH	LUNCH
16	BIOLOGY				LUNCH	LUNCH
17			SPANISH II			
18					ENGLISH 10	
19	PHYSICAL EDUCATION			SPANISH I		
20			PHYSICAL EDUCATION			SPANISH II
21		BIOLOGY LAB				
22					GEOMETRY	
23	AMERICAN HISTORY					
24						

Figure 3
Conventional Modular Schedule; Five-Day Cycle

	Monday	Tuesday	Wednesday	Thursday	Friday
1	ALG I	ALG I	ALG I	ALG I	ALG I
2	ALG I	ALG I	ALG I	ALG I	ALG I
3	ENG I	ENG I	ENG I	ENG I	ENG I
4	ENG I	ENG I	ENG I	ENG I	ENG I
5	P.E.	STUDY	P.E.	STUDY	STUDY
6	P.E.	STUDY	P.E.	STUDY	STUDY
7	P.E.	S LAB	P.E.	STUDY	S LAB
8	SCI	S LAB	SCI	SCI	S LAB
9	SCI	S LAB	SCI	SCI	SCI
10	LUNCH	LUNCH	LUNCH	LUNCH	LUNCH
11	SPAN	SPAN	SPAN	SPAN	SPAN
12	SPAN	SPAN	SPAN	SPAN	SPAN
13	STUDY	STUDY	STUDY	STUDY	STUDY
14	HIST	HIST	HIST	HIST	HIST
15	HIST	HIST	HIST	HIST	HIST

weeks; others as often as monthly. When these capabilities exist, the inherent flexibility is safeguarded.

Even without computer capabilities, however, principals who continue to operate with traditional schedules have introduced variety in their schedules by rotating or interchanging the periods. In Figure 4, an eight-period, five-day cycle schedule has been modified so that subjects fall in different time frames throughout the week. The interchange rotates throughout the

22

Figure 4
Rotating Period Schedule; Five-Day Cycle

	Monday	Tuesday	Wednesday	Thursday	Friday
1	A	C	E	G	B
2	B	D	F	H	C
3	C	E	G	A	D
4	D	F	H	B	E
5	E	G	A	C	F
6	F	H	B	D	G
7	G	A	C	E	H
8	H	B	D	F	A

Figure 5
A.M.-P.M. Rotating Period Schedule; Five-Day Cycle

	Monday	Tuesday	Wednesday	Thursday	Friday
1	A	B	C	D	B
2	B	C	D	A	C
3	C	D	A	B	D
4	D	A	B	C	A
5	E	F	G	H	F
6	F	G	H	E	G
7	G	H	E	F	H
8	H	E	F	G	E

23

schedule so that a student is as likely to have a subject first period on one day and last period on another.

Since total-cycle interchange is not always feasible in the comprehensive secondary school, a morning-afternoon interchange can be used (Figure 5). In this schedule, there is a separate and distinct interchange during the first four periods and another during the last four. A half-day rotation is useful when students are released either for a work-experience assignment or for afternoon attendance at a vocational-technical school. Part-time teachers can also more readily be utilized without conflicts.

VARIATIONS ON THE THEME

In addition to the traditional schedule, the flexible modular schedule, and their variations, a wide range of schedules exist which give vivid testimony to the ingenuity, creativity, and energy of school administrators and their university colleagues.

The following examples are but a sample of the scheduling formats found in schools throughout the United States and Canada.

Flexible Period—Five Day (Figure 6)

This schedule seeks to provide a variety of instructional time units within an otherwise conventional schedule. Length of period varies throughout the week to allow for both regular instruction and extended time for audiovisual presentations or group research projects.

Figure 6
Flexible Period Schedule; Five-Day Cycle

	Monday	Tuesday	Wednesday	Thursday	Friday
1	A	A	A	A	A
2	B	B	B	B	B
3	C	C	C	C	C
4	L	U	N	C	H
5	D	D	D	D	D
6	E	E	E	E	E
7	F	F	F	F	F

Activity Period, or Seven Over Six (Figure 7)

Within a 30-period week, this schedule has two multi-purpose periods (the X blocks) which can be used for field trips, cocurricular activities, large-group presentations, as period extenders, or occasionally for faculty inservice activities in conjunction with an early release of the student body. These X blocks (a "seventh" period) can be placed anywhere in the schedule, not necessarily back-to-back or on the same day. Note that a typical subject meets on four of the five days in the cycle but, because of the six-period day, for a longer time each day.

Figure 7
Activity Period—Seven Over Six Schedule

	Monday	Tuesday	Wednesday	Thursday	Friday
1	A	A	A	A	B
2	B	B	B	C	C
3	C	C	D	D	D
4	D	E	E	E	E
5	F	F	X	F	F
6	G	G	X	G	G

Single-Double Rotation (Figure 8)

Similar in some respects to the Flexible Period Schedule, the Single-Double Rotation Schedule calls for a subject to meet five periods during a five-day cycle, but on one day for two consecutive periods and not at all on another day. This kind of schedule works only if there are an even number of total periods per day.

Figure 8
Single-Double Rotation Schedule; Five-Day Cycle

	Monday	Tuesday	Wednesday	Thursday	Friday
1	A	A	A	A	B
2	A	B	B	B	B
3	C	C	C	D	C
4	D	C	D	D	D
5	E	E	E	E	F
6	F	F	E	F	F

Block of Time (Figure 9)

This example depicts part of a regular schedule to illustrate that two subjects, such as music and art, can meet for a double period two or three times a week. The pattern can vary on alternate weeks to provide equal time for each subject.

Figure 9
Block Schedule; Five-Day Cycle

	Monday	Tuesday	Wednesday	Thursday	Friday
1	ART	MUSIC	ART	MUSIC	ART
2	ART	MUSIC	ART	MUSIC	ART

26

Modified Block (Figure 10)

This is a modification of the basic block of time schedule in Figure 9. Music and art each meet for one single and two double blocks during the five-day cycle.

Figure 10
Modified Block Schedule; Five-Day Cycle

	Monday	Tuesday	Wednesday	Thursday	Friday
1	ART	MUSIC	ART	MUSIC	ART
2	ART	MUSIC	ART	MUSIC	MUSIC

SCHEDULING FOR INDIVIDUALIZATION

During the 1960s and 1970s, several sophisticated scheduling models were developed to permit schools to further individualize instruction while maintaining reasonable structure in the learning situation. Some of these models utilized block scheduling concepts, while others built upon the flexible modular schedule.

Fluid Block Schedule

In an effort to increase flexibility without loss of student accountability, some variations on the block schedule give a great deal of decision-making responsibility to the faculty members. One model, called the fluid block schedule (Ubben, 1976), groups students and teams of teachers for large segments of instructional time, up to three hours a day. Since the language arts and social studies programs are generally required in most schools, fluid blocks have frequently been constructed around these course areas.

Once the scheduler assigns a group of students to a particular team, the team designates an adviser for each youngster. The adviser helps each student plan a course of study for one-half of the school day that includes language arts, social studies, and electives in art, drama, driver's education, foreign language, mathematics, or music. The remainder of the school day consists of a more traditional program in courses such as algebra, chemistry, consumer economics, physics, typing, or—for vocationally-oriented students—a three-hour vocational-technical block.

The fluid block schedule may include open labs, individualized instruction, large groups, small groups, individual student activities, and mini-courses. The possible variations are almost unlimited, depending on the flexibility of teachers and the availability of open lab options.

Figure 11 shows the fluid block schedule and some of its variable elements.

Figure 11
Fluid Block Schedule

Basic Schedule

2 Language Arts + 2 Social Studies Teachers
Individualized Labs

		Music Lab	Math Lab	Driver's Education	Foreign Language	Art	Drama	Typing	Etc.
Hour 1 Hour 2 Hour 3	Fluid Block 100-120 Students								
Hour 4 Hour 5 Hour 6	1 hour elective 1 hour elective 1 hour elective	or		Three hour Vocational Block					

Mini-Course Schedule

3 Language Arts + 3 Social Studies Teachers
Individualized Labs

	LA	LA	SS	SS	LA	LA	SS	SS	LA	LA	SS	SS	Labs
Hour 1	Mini-Courses	Mini-Courses	Mini-Courses	Mini-Courses	Planning				Courses	Courses	Courses	Courses	Music Lab / Math Lab / Driver's Education / Foreign Language / Art / Drama
Hour 2					Mini-Courses	Mini-Courses	Mini-Courses	Mini-Courses	Planning				
Hour 3	Planning				Mini-Courses	Mini-Courses	Mini-Courses	Mini-Courses	Mini-	Mini-	Mini-	Mini-	

Large-Group, Small-Group, Individual Study Schedule

	Large-Group (120)				Individualized Labs
Small-Groups	15	15	15	15	
Small-Groups	15	15	15	15	(60)

28

Pontoon-Transitional Schedule

One of the earliest and most successful variations on the block of time schedule is the organizational pattern called the pontoon-transitional design (Georgiades, 1970). Intended to integrate two or more subjects from related or unrelated disciplines, this schedule utilizes teacher teams and teacher advisers to organize large-group presentations, small discussion groups, team teaching, and individual study in a flexible block of time. From two to six disciplines can be incorporated in a pontoon. (The term emphasizes the function of the schedule as a *bridge* to individualization.)

Typical pontoons are: art, English, and history; algebra II and chemistry; biology and physical education.

The basic pontoon is predicated on these formulas:

- Two Subjects/Teachers/Periods $= 2 \times$ Class Size $+ 10$
- Three Subjects/Teachers/Periods $= 3 \times$ Class Size $+ 10$

If class size is 30, a three-subject pontoon would have three teachers working with 100 students ($3 \times 30 + 10$) in three back-to-back class periods.

A school can employ one or more pontoons without disturbing the basic schedule of the school, and can add as many pontoons as desired. Ultimately, an entire school could be so organized.

Figure 12 illustrates a three-period pontoon for biology, English, and geometry. The students are organized into subgroups (A, B, C, etc.) of 12 or 13 students, and these groups are combined to form traditional or seminar groupings for the subject area activities.

Daily Demand Schedule

A complex variation of the flex-mod concept is the Daily Demand Schedule. This schedule changes in part every day, based on a weekly format developed by departmental teams working with a full-time coordinator. Some parts of the schedule are prescribed (office and "must" schedules); other parts are elective ("may" schedules). One of the more publicized examples of this schedule was implemented at Brookhurst Junior High School in the Anaheim, Calif., Union High School District. For detailed information, see *Instructional Programming* by Anthony Saville (1973).

Individualized Schedule

More flexible forms of scheduling customarily involve the reorganization of curriculum into continuous progress sequences, more time for individual projects, and a decrease in conventional class activities.

Several forms of individualized scheduling were developed during the NASSP Model Schools Project (1969-1974). These approaches combine office schedules (for large groups) with departmental and teacher-adviser guided schedules.

To schedule, a student meets with his or her adviser and works out a program based on a shortened version of the master schedule developed by the school staff. Scheduling is accomplished by some variation of the

Figure 12
Pontoon-Transitional Schedule

Day 1	11:55-12:00	12:05-1:20		1:25-2:35	
Biology	Large-Group	AB		CD	
English	Roll Call Only	12:05-12:40 CD	12:45-1:20 EF	1:25-1:55 AB	2:00-2:35 GH
Geometry		EF	CD	GH	AB
Directed Study		GH		EF	

Day 2	11:55-12:00	12:05-1:20		1:25-2:35	
Biology	Large-Group	EF		GH	
English	Roll Call Only	12:05-12:40 GH	12:45-1:20 CD	1:25-1:55 EF	2:00-2:35 AB
Geometry		CD	GH	AB	EF
Directed Study		AB		CD	

"arena" approach (students sign up for courses or exchange name cards for course cards). Independent/directed study takes place in "resource centers."

On the surface, individualized schedules resemble the typical flex-mods, but a major difference is that classes can start, end, and even be changed at any time (for a justifiable cause).

A master schedule excerpt from Pius X High School, Downey, Calif., is reproduced in Figure 13, and a sample student schedule from the same school appears in Figure 14. The mods are 30 minutes in length. These schedules were used during the Model Schools Project.

STANDARD AND STUDENT SELF-SCHEDULING (ARENA)

In addition to selecting from the smorgasbord of schedules available to a school system, school administrators and staff can promote active student participation through student self-scheduling.

Self-scheduling can best be understood by distinguishing between the two distinct phases of scheduling: the "build" or "generation" phase, and the "load" phase. These steps are interrelated, with the success of the latter highly dependent on the former.

30

The "build" phase consists of all the steps and procedures that add up to and include the construction of the master schedule. Particular components are: outlining the curriculum; printing the program of studies; conducting the registration process; interpreting course tallies; identifying course offerings and sections; determining staffing needs; assigning teachers to courses; analyzing conflict matrices; and building an efficient master schedule. This phase is the province of the scheduler and the school staff.

Upon completion of the "build" phase, the scheduler then "loads" or places students in the master schedule. Loading results in the production of individual student schedules. Students are assigned to specific sections of courses, at specific times of day, with specific teachers.

Student self-scheduling means full student involvement in the "load" phase of scheduling. Through a series of procedures (to be described in Chapter Four), students actually build their own schedules, taking into account a host of factors such as meeting times, assigned teachers, and potential conflicts with other courses.

Principals who strongly support the student self-scheduling concept acclaim its special advantages. Two of the most important advantages are the improvement in morale resulting from enhanced student decision-making responsibility, and the immediate resolution of most schedule conflicts (with the subsequent reduction of class changes in the fall).

Figure 13
Individualized Master Schedule Excerpt

Social Studies—Independent Study—Resource Center open all mods
Students should schedule 4 mods in the RC, one mod with a Subject
Consultant available (see below).

Social Studies Consultant
Available at the following times: Mon., 2, 7, 9, or 10; Tue., 1, 2, 10,
11, or 12; Wed., 6 or 11; Thur., 1, 2, 6, 7, 8, 11, or 12; Fri., 1, 5, 6,
10, 11, or 12.

Basic Sequence—Directed Study—Wed., 3-4 and Fri., 11-12
Prerequisite: Approval by Department Chairperson. Student must
schedule all 4 mods listed above.

Seminar: U.S. Government—Mon., 7-8 *or* Fri., 5-6
Prerequisite: completion of three U.S. Government units: Student
must schedule one of the 2-mod sets listed above.
Seminar: Psychology—Tues., 5-6 *or* Thur., 9-10
Prerequisite: completion of three Psychology units: Student must
schedule one of the 2-mod sets listed above.

Advanced Placement—U.S. History-set I—Mon., 2-3, Wed., 9-10,
Thur., 5-6
Prerequisite: completion of summer work assignment and approval of
subject consultant. Student must schedule all 6 mods listed above
and 6 mods in the Library.

Figure 14
Individualized Student Schedule

SCHEDULE GRID   **STUDENT NAME** __James Jones__

MOD	Monday	Tuesday	Wednesday	Thursday	Friday
1	T/A GRP.	RELIGION R.C.	PHOTO	PRAC. ARTS R.C.	MATH R.C.
2	BIOLOGY	RELIGION R.C.	PHOTO	PRAC. ARTS R.C.	MATH R.C.
3	BIOLOGY	LANGUAGE R.C.	PHOTO	PRAC. ARTS R.C.	LANGUAGE R.C.
4	BIOLOGY	BIOLOGY	ENGLISH R.C.	BIOLOGY	LANGUAGE R.C.
5	SOC. STUD. R.C.	BIOLOGY	BIOLOGY	BIOLOGY	BOOKKEEPING
6	LANGUAGE R.C.	MATH R.C.	BIOLOGY	BIOLOGY	SOC. STUD. R.C.
7	ENGLISH SEMINAR	ALGEBRA II	ENGLISH SEMINAR	ALGEBRA II	SOC. STUD. R.C.
8	ENGLISH SEMINAR	ALGEBRA II	ENGLISH SEMINAR	ALGEBRA II	LUNCH
9	LUNCH	LUNCH	LUNCH	LUNCH	ALGEBRA II
10	PRAC. ARTS R.C.	T.A.*	RELIGION SEMINAR	FINE ARTS R.C.	ALGEBRA II
11	ADV. SPORTS THEORY	ENGLISH R.C.	ADV. SPORTS THEORY	P.E.	LANGUAGE R.C.
12	ADV. SPORTS THEORY	RELIGION R.C.	ADV. SPORTS THEORY	P.E.	LANGUAGE R.C.

*Teacher adviser period for a personal advisement conference

Chapter Four

Preparing for the Master Schedule

ESTABLISHING THE SCHEDULING CALENDAR

AN EFFICIENT AND FLEXIBLE scheduling calendar is dependent on a school's basic scheduling model as well as several other factors. Schools that schedule completely by hand can set their own schedule and change it freely. When computerized techniques are used, however, coordination between the school and the data processing unit will somewhat fix the calendar of events.

The chief factors that determine the scheduling calendar are: complexity of the schedule; size of the student body and faculty; availability of budgetary information (staffing, etc.); standard versus student self-scheduling patterns; and finally, the date set for the distribution of student schedules. With regard to the latter, some schools like to hand out schedules in June (or earlier) for review and early adjustment, while others prefer to distribute them on the opening day of the fall term.

Scheduling is a year-long project for most schools. A typical calendar for a conventional secondary school might look like the following:

September-December—Review the curriculum and modify courses. Print the school's program of studies and prepare registration materials. Conduct the preregistration process.

January-February—Hold formal registration. Arrange for students to meet with counselors, department heads, and special subject teachers. Secure parents' approval of students' course selections.

February-March—Assemble enrollment information. After registration figures have been adjusted for cancelled and merged courses, determine staffing needs and submit for approval. Produce conflict matrix.

April—Construct the master schedule, either by hand or by machine.

May-June—For computerized scheduling, review initial computer simulation runs to determine whether the master schedule and/or student course selections must be modified. Contact students regarding conflicts. If scheduling is done by hand the master schedule should be reviewed to

33

determine its general efficiency for all students. Prepare student schedules by hand, as well as class, study hall, and homeroom lists.

July-August—Continue review of computerized simulations to increase the efficiency of the master schedule. Produce and distribute all schedules, lists, and reports to students and teachers.

The creation of the scheduling calendar must take into account factors peculiar to each locality. School schedulers need sufficient time to prepare the calendar each year, particularly in light of changing school conditions, past experience, and available staff. Turn-around time between the school and the processing bureau must be established. Nothing is more embarrassing to the scheduler than the absence of student schedules on opening day.

SETTING UP AND MAINTAINING FILES

The school scheduler must create specialized files for students, teachers, and courses. When computerized techniques are used, all needed files can be stored in the computer bank for easy access.

The scheduler begins by establishing a basic file for each student, sometimes referred to as the student master file, containing most or all of the following information:

- Student name, in full
- Student address
- Parent's address, if different
- Student computer identification number
- Telephone number
- Date of birth
- Sex

- Class or year of graduation
- Homeroom number
- Counselor's and/or teacher adviser's name
- House, if house plan is used
- Previous credits
- Grade point average
- Locker number.

Some schools may wish to gather additional information such as previous school attended, parish affiliation if a religious school, and type of academic program (college preparatory, commercial, or general).

Teacher files should contain all appropriate professional data, especially regarding subject certification. In a computerized system, teachers are usually given a number and a house plan assignment (if applicable). The scheduler will want to ensure that a current record is kept of every subject area for which the teacher is certified.

A file of all course offerings, usually referred to as "the course catalog," must be established for computerized scheduling. This listing assigns a number to each course, often with a predetermined code that contains such information as department, grade level, and degree of difficulty.

SCHEDULING PROCEDURES

Comprehensive scheduling procedures should be established so that everyone who must participate in the process—including administrators, guidance counselors, department heads, classroom teachers, students, parents, and the data processing unit members—knows the steps to be taken at various stages. Many of these procedures should appear in the school's program of studies and in the registration materials distributed to students and parents. An orientation meeting should be held for the staff.

New schedulers tend to inherit most procedures, and some procedures are dictated by the data processing unit. A useful strategy after completing a year's scheduling cycle is to meet with representative members of the faculty to review the previous year's experience, to document successful practices, and to identify areas needing improvement.

Several factors must be addressed in determining the appropriate scheduling procedures for a given school. Among these are: the costs related to the scheduling process; the type of scheduling procedures to be used—manual or computer-assisted; and whether student self-scheduling (arena) will be used.

Cost Analysis

Regardless of which scheduling method is used, a cost accrues to the school or school district. If the entire process is performed manually, the costs can be apportioned among administrative salaries, professional personnel salaries, clerical salaries, and supplies and materials.

Computerized scheduling costs are usually carried as a separate line item in the budget.

For those schools, districts, or municipalities with their own computers, computerized scheduling costs will probably be determined on a time-usage basis, plus a charge for materials and forms. The number of computer simulations after the master schedule has been built will also affect the cost.

When a school enters into a contract with a commercial data processing service bureau, the costs are determined by the nature of the scheduling package and the number of students processed. The more extensive the services requested—i.e., computer-built master schedule and computer loading of students—the greater the cost. Since the fees are ordinarily established on a per-pupil basis, a large school will pay more than a medium-sized school.

The principal or the scheduler must analyze the total costs of scheduling and ensure that they are included in the annual budget.

MANUAL OR COMPUTER-ASSISTED SCHEDULING

Many of the procedures employed in manual and computerized scheduling are the same. Steps requiring analysis and evaluation must be performed by the scheduler regardless of the method of scheduling. They include:

- Determining student needs
- Reviewing the curriculum
- Formulating the program of studies
- Preparing registration materials
- Setting the calendar for registration
- Interpreting the tallies
- Identifying staffing needs

- Utilizing a conflict matrix
- Building the master schedule.

The computer is most useful for the preparation and interpretation of a conflict matrix. A conflict matrix can be prepared by hand, but it is a very time consuming process and may take several years to revise. Many schedulers expedite the manual process by utilizing the services of a large group of students.

What is a conflict matrix and what purpose does it serve?

This valuable tool is a square array of all courses (or some, if preferred) for which potential conflicts are indicated. The matrix shows how many students have enrolled for pairs of courses in the curriculum. It lists, for example, how many students have signed up for honors chemistry and for Spanish III, for American history and for algebra II. (Using the matrix to build the master schedule is discussed in the next chapter.)

Computers tend to produce conflict matrices that display every course in the curriculum, although not all such data are essential. Generally, schedulers only need conflict information about courses with single sections (singletons), double sections (doubletons), or triple sections (tripletons). For this reason, preparing a conflict matrix by hand need not be an overwhelming task if, on average, only a moderate percentage of all courses being offered must be listed in the matrix.

Once the master schedule is built, significant differences do exist between manual and computerized scheduling approaches. Within the "load" phase, the computer will not only schedule each student more efficiently than can be done by hand, but it will also provide the scheduler with valuable reports to assist in refining both the master schedule and the process of scheduling.

Student Self-Scheduling (Arena)

In an earlier chapter, student self-scheduling (arena) was identified as an alternative method for completing the *load* phase of scheduling. When self-scheduling is used, it is for all practical purposes the concluding step of the process, since what remains is essentially clerical in nature.

Since most self-scheduling procedures are computerized, the following description assumes a computer-assisted process. A manual arena is also workable, using 3 × 5 cards, sign-up sheets, or other locally-prepared forms in place of computer cards.

The arena method of scheduling calls for students to take the place of the computer or the scheduling staff and "load themselves" into the master schedule. They do this by physically entering an arena (a gymnasium or other large site), picking up appropriate cards, signing their names on roster sheets, exchanging cards, or using some other prescribed method.

Staff and student orientation is critical to the success of the arena method. Key personnel (guidance counselors, department heads, and secretaries) must be fully informed about the entire process and capable of assisting students at any time. Pre-arena large and small-group review sessions are beneficial for students.

Arena approaches have a number of common elements. After staff members and students have been oriented to the arena methodology and timetable, the master schedule is distributed to students, along with a work sheet showing them how to construct at least *three* schedules. Alternative schedules are necessary because certain courses or sections may be closed when the student enters the arena. A schedule change may be necessary.

Variations exist in the logistics of arena scheduling. Seniors are usually scheduled first, followed by juniors, sophomores, etc. Within that pattern, groups of about 25 students are selected to enter the arena at prescribed intervals. A lottery system may be used, or homerooms may be selected at random. Another approach admits students to the arena according to the complexity of their schedules. Those with more singletons and doubletons enter first. Computer assistance is generally needed with this method.

The arena itself is usually organized on a departmental basis, with tables for required courses set up nearest the entrance. Guidance counselors are available for consultation, and are generally stationed in the center of the arena. Teachers and administrators circulate in the arena to assist students and to ensure a smooth flow of traffic.

Just prior to entering the arena, students visit a briefing room where procedures are summarized and closed courses or sections are announced or posted.

Students enter the arena and move from table to table, picking up cards (or signing course sheets) until they have built a complete conflict-free schedule.

Useful techniques for eliminating conflicts are the use of color-coded cards by subject or section, and a pre-check out table where an aide reviews the cards to ensure that students are properly scheduled. At this station, students may also be asked to write their names on subject cards, lest they later be misplaced. Some schools actually print student name cards to be exchanged for course cards. Students proceed to a final check-out table where their cards are deposited. Student cards are checked against the approved registration sheet and filed in some appropriate order.

Arena Models

With the diversity of philosophies found in schools and with increasingly sophisticated technological capabilities, it is not surprising that a variety of arena models exist. The choice of any particular model or the combination of two or more models is often left to the discretion of the scheduler.

- *Full-Arena Model*—Essentially the one described above, the full-arena model involves the entire student body in the process. The master schedule is a "demand" schedule, built primarily to meet the specific course requests of students.
- *College-Type Arena Model*—In the college style arena, the master schedule is predicated on past practices or faculty preferences. Students are required to "fit" themselves to the master schedule through the arena process. Many more student conflicts result in this approach.
- *Manual-Arena Model*—A manual method is used by schools that do not have access to a computer. Many of the strategies are similar to

computerized approaches, but students sign up for courses and sections on sheets of paper or locally produced forms (which, in turn, become the class lists).

- *Opening-Day Arena Model*—In school districts with a large turnover of students during the summer months (e.g., large urban schools and those near military installations), the arena process may take place just before the official opening of school. The greatest part of the master schedule is built based on projected enrollments, preliminary registrations, past practice, and accumulated experience. Modifications of the master schedule may be made during the arena process as new sections are added and others cancelled.

The opening-day arena is increasing in popularity for reasons of budget. Some school districts (such as those in California since the enactment of Proposition 13) have discovered that they cannot build the master schedule in the spring because the number of available teachers is not known until early summer. The opening-day arena offers a good compromise in these circumstances. Some work can be done on the master schedule, but final determination can be postponed until all pertinent information is available in the fall.

- *Arena-by-Exception Model*—This most recent modification of the arena method is a more restrictive use of the process. Schedulers can combine computer scheduling for some students with arena scheduling for others. The scheduler, for example, could decide that students in grades 9 and 10 will receive computer-determined schedules, while students in grades 11 and 12 will enter the arena. Other options permit students either to select a computer-determined schedule, to reject that entire schedule and enter the arena, or to accept part of the schedule and use the arena to resolve conflicts.

Arena Guidelines

The following general guidelines summarize the key elements of student self-scheduling:

1. Administration—Certain procedures have proved beneficial to the success of the arena process. A computer simulation should be run, where possible, to ensure the efficiency of the master schedule. Generally, arena scheduling calls for a master schedule which is at least 90 percent efficient for the major academic areas and at least 75 percent efficient for all required and elective courses. When this level is attained, either initially or following adjustments of the master schedule, the arena will achieve a high measure of success.

Students should always do their own scheduling. Only students absent because of prolonged illness or certain special education students should be allowed stand-ins. Students should be permitted to enter the arena only at the designated time, and to exit only when they have completed the process and returned all materials. Students should be required to select only those courses that appear on their registration sheets. All conflicts should be resolved in the arena. ''Conflict'' cards should be returned before new cards are selected. Once students leave the arena, they should not be allowed to return to adjust schedules.

2. Faculty Orientation—Since staff members may play different roles in the arena, all must understand the entire process, including use of the master schedule, the physical characteristics of the arena, the method of student entry, and the use of computer cards.

3. Student Orientation—Orientation usually takes place in class assemblies by year of graduation. These sessions should cover the following points:
- Pre-arena activities, such as registration and use of the master schedule to develop at least three alternative schedules;
- The basis for devising multiple schedules;
- The method of entry into the arena;
- The use of student name cards, subject cards, or sign-up sheets;
- The physical characteristics of the arena;
- The briefing room and its function;
- The check-in table and departmental tables;
- Closed and deleted sections;
- Availability of counselors, teachers, administrators, and aides;
- Course changes;
- Resolving conflicts;
- Pre-check-out and check-out tables;
- Procedures for absent students.

4. Incoming Students—The arena should preferably be set up at the "sending" school. (Busing is usually not very convenient.) If separate arenas are not feasible, a single arena at the high school is a workable alternative.

Arena Advantages and Disadvantages

Though strongly supported by schedulers throughout the country, arena scheduling has its pros and cons. Most often cited as advantages are the following:
- More decision-making responsibility is placed on the student;
- Communication between students and school staff members increases;
- Scheduling conflicts are resolved promptly;
- Significant reduction in fall schedule changes is achieved;
- Students display more enthusiasm toward the scheduling process;
- Counselors find they have more time for counseling.

Some disadvantages exist. Schools considering arena scheduling should ponder the following carefully before adopting the process:
- Faculty anxiety may result if students are allowed to select their teachers;
- Detailed planning and organization is needed to avoid disruptions;
- Additional staff time is needed during the arena, and this may increase costs;
- The arena may cause serious problems for schools with complex schedules;
- The computer does a better job of loading students.

Chapter Five
Building the Master Schedule

THERE ARE MANY WAYS in which a principal can demonstrate effectiveness and ability as the school's educational leader. Perhaps the most conspicuous exercise of leadership is the construction of an efficient master schedule. A smooth school opening provides clear evidence of a successful master schedule. A disorganized and confusing school opening often is attributable to a hastily built schedule.

A properly built master schedule is a painstakingly constructed instrument which unites curricular objectives, student course requests, and faculty strengths. The schedule also addresses such factors as physical facilities, time of day, and period of year.

A Balanced Master Schedule

A successful master schedule holds curricular objectives, student course requests, and faculty strengths and preferences in appropriate balance. Overemphasis on one area will have a restrictive effect on the others. Curriculum balance, for example, requires that in addition to a limited number of required courses, students be able to choose from a wide selection of elective offerings. For the college-bound, elective choices may be much narrower. Choice may lie between two laboratory sciences or two foreign languages. Similarly, during the first two years of high school, students are required to select courses from several departments, from various courses within the same department, and from differing levels of the same course.

When boards of education or individual departments prescribe a large number of required courses, students lose the flexibility to plan a program truly suited to their individual needs. When departments collectively or teachers individually press for scheduling preferences (time of day, specificity of course or section), the master schedule can lose its balance. In other words, the more the schedule reflects faculty preference for special assignments, the greater the potential for increased student conflicts.

Perhaps of even more consequence, student course requests must be balanced. Too many electives can result in a schedule replete with conflicts and faculty assignments that do not accommodate either teaching strengths or legitimate preferences. A scheduler in command is one who can maintain a proper and congenial balance among the various forces.

Choosing a Scheduling Model

The scheduling model chosen for a school should reflect both the curricular philosophy of the district/staff and the strengths of the local situation. Students can be scheduled in groups or individually. Block scheduling, for example, is used in many platoon elementary schools, middle schools, and junior high schools. Students with identical subjects are divided into the required number of sections and scheduled at different times in the day.

Consider a group of 150 students registered for the common subjects of English, science, mathematics, music, and history. One hundred fifty students can be divided into five blocks of 30, or six blocks of 25 each. Within a seven-period schedule, the first block of students could be placed in English during period 1, in science during period 2, in mathematics during period 4, in music during period 5, and in history during period 7. The next block could be assigned as follows: English—period 2, science—period 1, mathematics—period 5, music—period 3, and history—period 6. A similar pattern could be used for the remaining groups to avoid subject conflicts within periods. (See Chapter Three for scheduling models.)

When electives must be scheduled along with required courses in a block schedule, the schedule maker can use a partial block pattern. All required courses can be scheduled using the block method, while electives are placed into the remaining periods by a "mosaic" method (discussed below). Variations of the block can accommodate special groupings or a school-wide activity period (e.g., the fluid block, the pontoon-transitional schedule, and the common core schedule). The block schedule is most useful to place groups of students together for a large amount of time with a team of teachers. Elective courses usually demand individual loading methods.

Mosaic scheduling methods are concerned with individual sections of courses. Used in conjunction with a conflict matrix, the mosaic is most useful in high schools where required courses are offered in concert with a wide range of electives. Sometimes the block schedule approach is impractical when large groups of students do not take similar subjects. Special grouping within departments or a proliferation of semester-length courses, for example, may require the scheduler to place one course section at a time into the master schedule, continually building upon previous entries until the total mosaic is completed.

A common denominator of both block and mosaic approaches is an overriding concern to construct a schedule in which potential conflicts are minimized.

Interpreting Course Tallies and Assigning Teachers

The scheduling cycle requires an analysis of course tallies so that a basic equation is satisfied: The number of course sections offered to students must equal the number of teacher sections available.

Several observations about course tally interpretation can be made. Whether set by the board of education, the central office, the teacher contract, or at the discretion of the principal, a figure must be set representing average class size, and this figure must be consistently used in determining sections. A minimum course enrollment number must also be established. For specialized courses such as industrial arts, business education, or art, however, different guidelines can be employed. A typing room may hold 75 students, while an electronics lab may hold only 18. All cut-off points should be known and enforced by both administrators and faculty members to avoid any semblance of preferential treatment.

When the scheduler, with staff input, has balanced teachers and sections, teachers can be assigned to sections. Differentiated staffing assignments must be accounted for, specifications of the teacher contract addressed, and a teacher assignment sheet prepared.

Table 1 illustrates a teaching assignment schedule in a typical high school. In this example, each teacher is assigned five course sections requiring no more than three distinct preparations. A complete assignment sheet would contain all departments and teachers in the left column, and every section of every course in the array to the right. As much as possible, these assignments should reflect the individual strengths of teachers as well as their stated preferences. The scheduler might also develop a list of alternative assignments for each course in the event that master schedule reconstruction dictates reassignment of some teachers to avoid conflicts.

The Conflict Matrix

Even in the best-organized scheduling process numerous "conflicts" can arise. Conflicts can occur about rooms, programs, and courses to be dropped or merged. The most common student conflict arises when two of a student's preferred courses are scheduled in the same period. If a single section course (singleton) is placed in a particular period along with another single section course, students will be unable to schedule one of them.

Conflicts do not arise so much from individual student preferences as from the difficulty of constructing a schedule that will accommodate the seemingly infinite combinations of different courses. The scheduler's goal for each scheduling cycle (year or semester) is the building of an efficient schedule that is as conflict-free as possible. With few potential conflicts, only a small number of students will need to change their course requests.

The conflict matrix was described in Chapter Four as a *square array of all courses in the curriculum paired against each other*. An example of an early computer-produced matrix is shown in Figure 1.

Increased competition among producers of computer scheduling packages has resulted in improved conflict matrices. Figures 2 and 3 illustrate two alternatives.

The matrices in these two figures are a marked improvement over that in Figure 1. Not only is there a saving in the amount of computer paper consumed in the process, but only those courses for which a potential conflict exists are exhibited. There is less to read and interpret, and the read-outs are easier to handle.

Table 1
Partial Teacher Assignment Schedule

DEPARTMENT	TEACHER	ASSIGNMENTS
English	Comma, A.	2—Composition; 1—Short Story; 2—Poetry
	Duce, L.	1—English 10A; 3—English 9; 1—Theater
	Poetic, W.	2—Poetry; 3—Drama
	Test, A.	1—English 12; 2—Film; 2—American Literature
Mathematics	Divisor, A.	3—Algebra I; 2—Basic Mathematics
	Graph, B.	2—Geometry; 2—Algebra II; 1—Calculus
	Tablish, S.	3—Computer Programing; 2—Functions/Relations
Science	Beaker, A.	3—Earth Science; 2—Oceanography
	Burner, B.	4—Biology; 1—Chemistry
Business	Margin, W.	2—Typing I; 2—Stenography II; 2—Transcription
	Typo, A.	3—Office Procedures; 2—Typing II
Industrial Arts	Carpenter, A.	3—Metalworking I; 2—Metalworking II
	Wood, H.	2—Woodworking I; 2—Woodworking II; 1—Woodworking III

end of file 14

Figure 1
Traditional Computer Conflict Matrix

	1	2	3	4	5	6	7	8	9	10	11	12	13	14	15	16	17	18	19	20	21	22	23	24	25	26	27	28	29	30	31	32	33	34	
Instr Music	48	4	4	1	–	–	–	–	1	–	–	–	–	4	–	–	3	1	8	8	2	1	1	–	4	4	1	2	5	5	3	1	–	1	1
Creative Writing	4	36	15	–	1	–	1	1	1	1	–	–	1	5	4	–	1	1	18	17	3	1	1	–	–	–	3	–	11	5	1	–	–	–	2
Calculus	4	15	18	14	–	–	–	–	1	1	1	–	–	–	–	–	–	–	15	2	1	–	–	–	–	1	1	–	6	–	1	–	–	–	3
Functions/Relations	1	–	1	14	–	–	–	–	1	–	1	–	–	–	–	–	–	–	1	–	–	–	–	–	–	1	1	–	6	–	1	–	–	–	4
Italian 12	–	1	–	–	16	15	1	–	2	1	1	–	–	–	3	2	–	–	1	1	–	–	3	–	–	11	–	1	–	–	–	–	5	–	5
Clerical Practices	–	–	–	–	15	16	1	6	–	–	–	–	–	6	–	–	–	–	–	–	–	–	–	–	–	–	1	–	–	–	–	–	–	–	6
Adv Sculpt	–	–	–	–	1	1	16	6	2	–	–	–	–	–	–	–	–	–	–	–	–	–	3	–	–	–	2	–	1	–	1	–	–	1	7
Arch Drafting	–	1	–	–	–	6	6	6	–	–	–	–	–	–	–	–	–	2	1	1	1	–	1	–	–	–	2	–	2	–	1	–	–	–	8
Adv Ceramics	1	1	1	1	2	–	2	–	20	1	–	–	–	–	1	–	–	2	2	2	1	2	1	1	1	–	2	1	2	–	–	1	1	–	9
Electronics 10	–	1	1	–	1	–	–	–	1	17	–	–	–	–	–	–	–	2	1	–	3	–	3	–	–	–	1	3	2	–	–	3	3	1	10
English 10 A	–	–	1	1	1	–	–	–	–	–	18	–	–	–	8	–	6	–	–	–	–	–	–	–	–	–	2	–	3	–	–	–	–	–	11
English 10 B	–	–	–	–	–	–	–	–	–	–	–	20	–	–	–	–	–	–	–	–	–	–	–	1	–	–	3	–	–	–	–	–	–	–	12
Mus Harmony	–	1	–	–	–	–	–	–	–	–	–	–	5	5	–	–	–	–	–	–	–	–	–	–	–	–	1	1	–	–	–	–	–	–	13
Mus Theory	4	5	–	–	–	6	–	–	–	–	–	–	5	6	6	–	–	–	–	–	–	–	–	–	–	–	–	–	–	–	–	–	–	–	14
Adv Instr Music	–	4	–	–	3	–	–	–	1	–	8	–	–	6	35	1	–	1	–	–	2	2	2	–	1	5	–	3	–	2	–	3	1	1	15
Italian 10	1	–	–	–	2	–	–	–	–	–	–	–	–	–	1	14	6	2	–	–	–	–	–	1	–	7	–	1	–	3	1	1	1	1	16
Music History	3	1	–	–	–	–	–	–	–	–	6	–	–	–	–	6	6	2	1	–	–	2	2	–	1	–	2	1	1	–	1	–	1	1	17
Automotive*	1	1	–	–	–	–	–	2	2	2	–	–	–	–	1	2	2	42	1	2	–	2	2	2	1	–	1	1	–	–	–	1	5	3	18
Physics	8	18	15	1	1	–	–	1	2	1	–	–	–	–	–	–	1	1	35	15	7	–	1	–	3	–	3	3	3	1	–	1	–	–	19
Adv Math	8	17	2	–	1	–	–	1	2	–	–	–	–	–	–	–	–	2	15	44	7	1	2	1	3	–	1	1	1	–	1	–	1	–	20
Com Science II*	2	3	1	–	–	–	–	1	1	3	–	–	–	–	2	–	–	–	7	7	20	–	2	–	1	–	3	1	–	1	–	1	–	1	21
Office Practices	1	1	–	–	–	–	–	–	2	–	–	–	–	–	2	–	2	2	–	1	–	35	–	1	–	–	2	–	8	–	4	2	4	3	22
Wood 10	1	1	–	–	3	–	3	1	1	3	–	–	–	–	2	–	2	2	1	2	2	–	32	3	–	–	2	5	3	–	4	2	4	3	23
Bus Comm.	–	–	–	–	–	–	–	–	1	–	–	1	–	–	–	1	–	2	–	1	–	1	3	41	–	–	5	1	3	1	6	1	4	1	24
Algebra II	4	–	–	–	–	–	–	–	1	–	–	–	–	–	1	–	1	1	3	3	1	–	–	–	39	–	2	1	5	–	4	–	4	–	25
Italian 9	4	–	1	1	11	–	–	–	–	–	–	–	–	–	5	7	–	–	–	–	–	–	–	–	–	38	2	1	6	1	1	–	2	1	26
Mech Drafting	1	3	1	1	–	1	2	2	2	1	2	3	1	–	–	–	2	1	3	1	3	2	2	5	2	2	28	1	6	1	1	–	1	1	27
Algebra 10	2	–	–	–	1	–	–	–	1	3	–	–	1	–	3	1	1	1	3	1	1	–	5	1	1	1	1	82	6	1	–	1	1	–	28
Com Science I*	5	11	6	6	–	–	1	2	2	2	3	–	–	–	–	–	1	–	3	1	–	8	3	3	5	6	6	6	51	1	2	1	2	1	29
French 9	5	5	–	–	–	–	–	–	–	–	–	–	–	–	2	3	–	–	1	–	1	–	–	1	–	1	1	1	1	55	–	2	–	–	30
Geometry	3	1	1	1	–	–	–	1	–	–	–	–	–	–	–	3	1	–	–	1	–	4	4	6	4	1	1	–	2	–	60	2	1	1	31
Electronics 9	1	–	–	–	–	–	–	–	1	3	–	–	–	–	3	1	–	1	1	–	1	2	2	1	–	–	–	1	1	2	2	40	1	1	32
Ceramics	–	–	–	–	5	–	–	–	1	3	–	–	–	–	1	1	1	5	–	1	–	4	4	4	4	2	1	1	2	–	1	1	64	1	33
Machine Shop	1	–	–	–	–	–	1	–	–	1	–	–	–	–	1	1	1	3	–	–	1	3	3	1	–	1	1	–	1	–	1	1	1	55	34

Figure 2
Alternative Conflict Matrix A
Potential Course Conflicts
Central High School

Number	Name	Sections	Requests	Number	Name	Sections	Requests	Potential Conflicts
405	Spanish IV	1	18	099	Lunch	3	90	1
				104	English Literature	1	25	1
				104	American Literature	1	24	1
				704	Drama I	1	23	1
				704	Drama II	1	23	1
				903	Girl's PE III & IV	2	46	1
416	French IV	1	22	099	Lunch	3	90	2
				104	English Literature	1	25	2
				104	American Literature	1	24	1
				204	Economics	1	25	2
				504	Trigonometry	1	23	2
				504	Analysis	1	23	2
				604	Physics	1	23	2
				701	Band	1	100	12
				903	Boy's PE III & IV	2	56	11
				903	Girl's PE III & IV	2	46	11
511	Algebra I	4	110	099	Lunch	3	90	8
				101	English I	2	38	8
				201	World History	2	48	4
				202	American History	2	48	4
				601	Typing I	1	24	2
				601	Typing II	1	24	2
				602	Shorthand I	1	14	2
				602	Shorthand II	1	14	2
				701	Band	1	100	3
				703	Art I	1	24	2
				801	Woodworking Shop	1	14	2
				901	Boy's PE I	1	34	4
				901	Girl's PE I	1	34	4
521	Geometry	4	103	099	Lunch	3	90	8
				102	English II	2	38	8
				201	World History	2	48	4
				202	American History	2	48	4
				401	Spanish I	1	22	2
				401	French I	1	23	2
				602	Biology	2	47	7
				603	Chemistry	1	27	1
				601	Typing I	1	24	2

Figure 3
Alternative Conflict Matrix B

SAMPLE CONFLICT MATRIX

| UNIVERSAL HIGH SCHOOL | SCHOOL YEAR 1982-83 | DATE 2/15/82 |

COURSE NAME/NUMBER	POTENTIAL CONFLICTS WITH	COURSE NAME/NUMBER
CREATIVE WRITING—115	15	CALCULUS—212
	17	ADV. MATH—228
ENGLISH 10A—126	1	ITALIAN 12—318
ENGLISH 10B—127	1	INSTR. MUSIC—601
CALCULUS—212	15	CREATIVE WRITING—115
	1	FUNCT/RELAT—216
FUNCT/RELAT—216	1	CALCULUS—212
	1	PHYSICS—445
ADV. MATH—228	17	CREATIVE WRITING—115
	2	CALCULUS—212
GEOMETRY—233	1	ITALIAN 12—318
	3	INSTR. MUSIC—601
ITALIAN 12—318	1	CREATIVE WRITING—115
	1	ENGLISH 10A—126

POTENTIAL CONFLICTS WITH	COURSE NAME/NUMBER
1	ITALIAN 12—318
18	PHYSICS—445
8	ADV. INSTR. MUSIC—607
2	ADV. MATH—228
15	PHYSICS—445
1	INSTR. MUSIC—601
3	ADV. INSTR. MUSIC—607
1	ITALIAN 12—318
15	PHYSICS—445
2	MUSIC THEORY—603
1	ADV. MATH—228
1	GEOMETRY—233

Because many computer programs produce a matrix similar to that in Figure 1, and because this format would be used in a manually developed matrix, we will use a modification of it for our discussion of schedule building.

In Figure 1, every piece of information appears twice. In a multiplication table, the product of 3×5 is 15, as is the product of 5×3. In Figure 1, note the number 15 at the intersection of row 19 (physics) and of column 3 (calculus). This same number "15" is found at the intersection of row 3 (calculus) and column 19 (physics). In either case, 15 represents the number of students enrolled in both calculus and physics. If only one section of each course is offered and if both sections are scheduled in the same period, 15 students will have a conflict. These students will not be able to take both courses unless one is rescheduled.

This method of "reading" the matrix to anticipate potential conflicts is used throughout the process. Although different implications arise when comparing two-section courses (doubletons) as opposed to singletons, the matrix maintains a high degree of usefulness. The absence of a number in the matrix—usually shown as a dash, a zero, or a blank space—indicates that no students are registered for both courses. No conflict is present, for example, when a course taken exclusively by freshmen is compared with a course offered only to seniors. In these instances, the scheduler can schedule the two courses during the same period without problem, as long as teachers and rooms are available.

Note that the conflict matrix in Figure 1 has an obvious diagonal running from the upper left to the lower right corner. This diagonal represents the intersection of each course with itself, and as such is a convenient indicator of the enrollment.

During the sample building of a master schedule that follows, we will use an abbreviated version of a conflict matrix (see Figure 4). Keep in mind that an actual conflict matrix would probably be at least twice the size of this example.

Some schedulers prefer to build a conflict matrix by hand. One common method employs paraprofessionals to examine the registration sheets and post potential conflicts on a large chart. Actually, the only courses needed on the chart are singletons, doubletons, and tripletons. A cumulative record of possible conflicts is kept as each student's registration card is examined; the totals for each pair of courses are entered on the chart. Separate charts may be used to compare singleton courses with other singletons, singletons with doubletons, doubletons with doubletons, singletons with tripletons, doubletons with tripletons, and tripletons with tripletons. If a single chart is utilized, singletons should be placed first, followed by doubletons, then tripletons.

Many schedulers use students to help complete a conflict matrix. Students are given a manageable number of cards and are asked by the adult in charge to analyze the number of potential conflicts on the registration cards for each pair of courses. One of the students records the data on the chart, adding the conflict totals after all pairings have been tallied.

Whatever method is used for a conflict matrix—machine or manual—

47

Figure 4
Abbreviated Conflict Matrix

	ENGLISH 10	ENGLISH 11	ENGLISH 12	POETRY 2	U.S. HISTORY	WORLD HISTORY	SOCIOLOGY	ECONOMICS	SPANISH 1	SPANISH 2	SPANISH 3	CHEMISTRY	BIOLOGY 10	EARTH SCIENCE	ALGEBRA 1	ALGEBRA 2	DIST. EDUC.	KEYBOARDING	BUS. MACHINES	STENO 1	DRAFTING 1	DRAFTING 2	CONS. EDUC.	FOODS 1	FOODS 2	CHILD DEVEL.
CHILD DEVEL.		2	1															3					2	5	1	
FOODS 2		6	6	2												7		7						14		
FOODS 1	11	3	1									2						2	5				4			
CONS. EDUC.		4	2		1													12	8							
DRAFTING 2	5	13	8			2		1				5	3			4		8								
DRAFTING 1	2	8			3		1					7	2			1	7	2	4							
STENO 1		3	3															2								
BUS. MACHINES		3	4			1							3					13								
KEYBOARDING	5	11	12	1									5													
DIST. EDUC.		4	6																							
ALGEBRA 2	33	5	2		3	1	1						8	5	16											
ALGEBRA 1	2								12	18			3	11												
EARTH SCIENCE	3								23																	
BIOLOGY 10	41								15																	
CHEMISTRY		17	3	1	11	5	3	2			12															
SPANISH 3	1	18	7	4	7	2		3																		
SPANISH 2	10	6				3																				
SPANISH 1	2																									
ECONOMICS			10	12																						
SOCIOLOGY			15	3																						
WORLD HISTORY		21																								
U.S. HISTORY	28																									
POETRY 2																										
ENGLISH 12																										
ENGLISH 11																										
ENGLISH 10																										

only the number of potential conflicts are listed, not student names. Individual student conflicts are determined either by separate computer printout or by comparing course lists.

Organizing the Conflict Matrix

Several general principles are helpful in constructing a conflict matrix. All singletons should be listed first, then doubletons, and finally tripletons. The ordering of singletons should be based on some consistent criteria. Many schedulers list the singletons with the greatest number of potential conflicts first, followed by those with progressively lower potential for conflict. Other schedulers rank the singletons in an order that represents the "importance" of the courses as perceived by the scheduler and/or a scheduling committee. A combination of both methods may be used.

Scheduling efficiency is enhanced if the following order is observed in placing sections into the master schedule:

1. All restrictive situations
2. Unrestricted singletons
3. Unrestricted doubletons
4. Unrestricted tripletons
5. Unrestricted courses with four or more sections.

Restrictive situations are sections of courses that must meet at specified times because of the nature of the courses (i.e., band, work experience/work study); the use of a part-time or shared-time teacher; a specialized team-teaching situation; the limitations of a particular room; or a unique multi-period arrangement. Preferential teaching assignments are restrictions. A department head, for example, may prefer to teach a particular class at a particular time, or a coach may ask for a planning period at the end of the day to prepare for the arrival of the team. Unrestricted courses/sections are those which can be placed anywhere in the schedule.

Relatively few materials are needed to build the master schedule. Pencils, paper or large pieces of cardboard, a ruler or straight edge, and erasers are essential. An adding machine with tape is also helpful. Large magnetic or non-magnetic master schedule boards can be purchased from a variety of manufacturers. Personal scheduling books are handy (See Figures 26 and 27).

There are several ways to set up the schedule depending, of course, on its complexity. For a conventional schedule, one can organize a chart like that shown in Figure 5. The periods are listed horizontally across the top of the chart and the faculty, by department, are arranged vertically, usually in alphabetical order. Teachers assigned to two or more departments can be scheduled in the department where they teach most of their courses, or can be listed in both departments. For semester courses, the chart can be separated into two sections, one on the left for the first semester and one on the right for the second semester.

A number of elements affect the scheduler's ability to construct a schedule with a minimum of conflicts. Some of these are:

1. Complex schedules such as flex-mod or individualized variations.

Figure 5

Building the Master Timetable

Timetable Construction Using the Conflict Matrix

	1	2	3	4	5	6	7
English A Say, S.							
English B Talics, I.							
Math A Visor, D.							
Math B Dition, A.							
Math C Quasion, E.							
Science A Sotope, I.							
Mod. Lang. A Ography, G.							
Mod. Lang. B Kline, D.							
Business A Typo, A.							
Business B Fishent, E.							
Tech. A Lectric, E.							
Tech. B Square, T.							
Tech. C Clamp, C.							
Art A Tale, D.							
Music A Sing, I.							

2. High subject density within the schedule—e.g., six required courses in a six-period schedule.
3. A proliferation of semester, trimester, or quarter courses.
4. An excessive number of singletons.
5. Nongraded courses (those open to students in several grade levels; e.g., sixth, seventh, and eighth graders).
6. A large number of restrictive factors: part-time faculty, etc.
7. Constraints in the teacher contract.
8. Many teachers assigned to more than one department.
9. Many double-period subjects, such as science labs.

The greater the number of these factors present, the more difficult it will be to build a conflict-reduced schedule.

Constructing the Course Schedule

A workable conflict matrix demands a systematic scheduling process. No "seat of the pants," "trial and error," or other haphazard method will work. The following example is illustrative of a scheduling technique that has proven its efficiency in numerous schools and with countless schedules. For the sake of economy and ease of understanding, we will use a "micro-schedule" with only 15 courses to form the sample matrix. (Most actual schedules will have many more.) Ten courses are singletons, three are doubletons, and two are tripletons.

Step 1.

The initial step in the conflict matrix is determining the TOTAL CONFLICTS *by adding across each row* of the computerized (or manual) conflict tallies. Note that the number on the main diagonal is *not* included in the total, since that number is the intersection of a course with itself. Courses with one asterisk are singleton courses; those with two asterisks are doubletons; courses with three asterisks are tripletons. The course entitled Creative Writing is team taught. (See Figure 6.)

Step 2.

After determining the total conflicts, *rank order* the singleton, doubleton, and tripleton conflicts separately, from highest subtotal to lowest subtotal. Recall that effective master schedule construction requires singletons to be scheduled first, followed by doubletons, tripletons, etc. Within each category, the course with the highest number of potential conflicts is usually scheduled first, then the next highest, etc. (See Figure 7.) The "Total Conflicts" column indicates that Creative Writing, with 56, is the highest conflict singleton; Instrumental Music, with 39, is next. The lowest conflict singleton is English 10B, with one conflict. Physics is the highest doubleton, with 57 total conflicts.

Step 3.

Often a scheduler must make certain *accommodations*, referred to earlier as "restrictive situations." Either a course or a teacher, or both, must be scheduled at a particular time. The restrictions must be accommodated at

Figure 6

PERIOD(S) ASSIGNED
SCHEDULING RANK++
TOTAL CONFLICTS

Course Name/Number	115	126	127	212	216	228	233	318	340	445	534	541	601	603	607
TOTAL CONFLICTS	56	9	1	37	6	44	6	8	7	57	5	7	39	6	20
607 ADV. INSTR. MUSIC*	1	8		3		3	1			2					35
603 MUSIC THEORY*												2	4	6	
601 INSTR. MUSIC*	4			4	1	8			5	8	3		48	4	
541 OFF. PRAC.**								1			3	35		2	
534 CLER. PRAC.*											15	3	3		
445 PHYSICS**	18			15	1	15				35			8		
340 FRENCH 9***								1	55				5		
318 ITALIAN 12*		1					3	16	1			1			
233 GEOMETRY***							60	3							1
228 ADV. MATH**	17			2	1	44				15			8		3
216 FUNCTIONS/RELATIONS*					14	1				1			1		
212 CALCULUS*	15			18		2				15			4		3
127 ENGLISH 10B*		1	20												
126 ENGLISH 10A*		18	1					1							8
115 CREATIVE WRITING*+	36			15		17				18			4		1

*Singleton
**Doubleton
***Tripleton

+Team taught
++Follows order recommended on page _____ :
singletons first, then doubletons, etc.

Figure 7

Course	115	126	127	212	216	228	233	318	340	445	534	541	601	603	607
PERIOD(S) ASSIGNED															
SCHEDULING RANK++	1	5	10	3	7	12	15	6	14	11	9	13	2	8	4
TOTAL CONFLICTS	56	9	1	37	6	44	6	8	7	57	5	7	39	6	20
607 ADV. INSTR. MUSIC*	1	8	—	—	3	—	—	3	1	—	2	2	—	—	35
603 MUSIC THEORY*	—	—	—	—	—	—	2	—	—	—	—	—	4	6	—
601 INSTR. MUSIC*	4	—	1	4	1	8	3	—	5	8	—	1	48	4	—
541 OFF. PRAC.**	—	—	—	—	—	—	—	—	—	—	3	35	1	—	2
534 CLER. PRAC.*	—	—	—	—	—	—	—	—	—	—	15	3	—	—	2
445 PHYSICS**	18	—	—	15	1	15	—	—	—	35	—	—	8	—	—
340 FRENCH 9***	—	—	—	—	—	—	—	1	55	—	—	—	5	—	1
318 ITALIAN 12*	1	1	—	—	—	1	1	16	1	—	—	—	—	—	3
233 GEOMETRY***	—	—	—	—	—	—	60	1	—	—	—	—	3	2	—
228 ADV. MATH**	17	—	—	2	1	44	—	1	—	15	—	—	8	—	—
216 FUNCTIONS/RELATIONS*	—	—	—	1	14	1	—	—	—	—	—	—	1	—	3
212 CALCULUS*	15	—	—	18	1	2	—	—	—	15	—	—	4	—	—
127 ENGLISH 10B*	—	—	20	—	—	—	—	—	—	—	—	—	1	—	—
126 ENGLISH 10A*	—	18	—	—	—	—	—	1	—	—	—	—	—	—	8
115 CREATIVE WRITING*+	36	—	—	15	—	17	—	1	—	18	—	—	4	—	1

Course Name/Number

CREATIVE WRITING*+ — 115
ENGLISH 10A* — 126
ENGLISH 10B* — 127
CALCULUS* — 212
FUNCTIONS/RELATIONS* — 216
ADV. MATH** — 228
GEOMETRY*** — 233
ITALIAN 12* — 318
FRENCH 9*** — 340
PHYSICS** — 445
CLER. PRAC.* — 534
OFF. PRAC.** — 541
INSTR. MUSIC* — 601
MUSIC THEORY* — 603
ADV. INSTR. MUSIC* — 607

*Singleton
**Doubleton
***Tripleton

+Team taught
++Follows order recommended on page _____ : singletons first, then doubletons, etc.

Figure 8

Course Name/Number	115	126	127	212	216	228	233	318	340	445	534	541	601	603	607
PERIOD(S) ASSIGNED	—	7	—	—	—	—	—	—	—	—	—	—	—	—	—
SCHEDULING RANK++	1	5	10	3	7	12	15	6	14	11	9	13	2	8	4
TOTAL CONFLICTS	56	9	1	37	6	44	6	8	7	57	5	7	39	6	20
607 ADV. INSTR. MUSIC*	1	8	—	—	3	8	—	3	—	—	2	2	8	35	—
603 MUSIC THEORY*	—	—	—	—	—	—	—	—	—	—	—	2	4	6	35
601 INSTR. MUSIC*	4	—	—	4	—	1	—	1	5	8	3	—	48	4	8
541 OFF. PRAC.**	—	—	—	—	—	—	—	—	1	—	3	35	—	2	2
534 CLER. PRAC.*	—	—	—	—	—	—	—	—	—	—	15	3	3	—	2
445 PHYSICS**	18	—	—	15	—	15	—	1	—	35	—	—	8	—	—
340 FRENCH 9***	—	—	—	—	—	—	—	—	55	—	—	1	5	—	—
318 ITALIAN 12*	1	1	—	—	1	—	—	16	—	1	—	—	1	—	3
233 GEOMETRY***	—	—	—	—	—	—	60	1	—	—	3	2	—	—	—
228 ADV. MATH**	17	—	—	2	1	44	—	—	—	15	—	—	1	—	8
216 FUNCTIONS/RELATIONS*	—	—	—	1	14	1	—	1	—	—	—	—	—	—	3
212 CALCULUS*	15	—	—	18	1	2	—	—	—	15	—	—	4	—	—
127 ENGLISH 10B*	—	—	20	—	—	—	—	—	—	—	—	—	—	—	—
126 ENGLISH 10A*	—	18	—	—	—	—	—	1	—	—	—	—	—	—	8
115 CREATIVE WRITING*+	36	—	—	15	—	17	—	1	—	18	—	—	4	—	1

+Team taught
++Follows order recommended on page _____:
singletons first, then doubletons, etc.

*Singleton
**Doubleton
***Tripleton

54

this stage of the process. Calculus, for example, may be slotted for Period 7 because the teacher is only available at that time. Note this in the "Period Assigned" column. (See Figure 8.)

Singletons

Step 4.

The scheduler is now ready to identify the potential conflicts in the matrix. Starting with the highest ranked unscheduled singleton (Creative Writing-115 in the sample matrix), try to assign each course to a period that is free of conflicts. (Later when we are well into the process and no conflict-free periods exist, we will usually choose the period with the *fewest* conflicts. Should a different choice be dictated by local considerations, the scheduler must make the appropriate choice of period.)

The potential conflicts with a course or section of a course previously assigned are identified in a simple chart, recording them by period (Figure 9). First read across the Creative Writing-115 line (or down the corresponding column). Enter into the chart the number of conflicts possible each period. At this stage, the only potential conflicts are between Creative Writing-115 and Calculus-212. Since Calculus is scheduled in period 7, the 15 potential conflicts should be noted at that period. (In these first few samples, too few courses will have been scheduled to create any real scheduling problems.) Pursue this methodology from first course to last. As more courses are assigned, the conflict-free choices are reduced.

Figure 9

Course: Creative Writing—115

Period	1	2	3	4	5	6	7
Possible Conflicts							15

Since Creative Writing would conflict only with period 7, it can be scheduled in any period from 1 to 6. The scheduler, noting that this is a team-taught course, schedules it for period 2, respecting a "local agreement" that both teachers assigned to the course will have common planning and preparation during period 1. (See Figure 10.)

We will show only the line under consideration in the remaining illustrations of the conflict resolution process (Figures 11 through 18, and 20 through 22). The entire matrix will be shown again in Figures 19 and 23.

Step 5.

The next singleton to be scheduled is Instrumental Music-601. There are four potential conflicts with Calculus (assigned to Period 7), and four with Creative Writing (assigned to period 2). Analysis of the matrix shows this pattern of conflict. (See Figure 10 for the entire matrix.)

Figure 10

	115	126	127	212	216	228	233	318	340	445	534	541	601	603	607
PERIOD(S) ASSIGNED	2	—	—	—	—	—	—	—	—	—	—	—	7	—	—
SCHEDULING RANK++	1	5	10	3	7	12	15	6	14	11	9	13	2	8	4
TOTAL CONFLICTS	56	9	1	37	6	44	6	8	7	57	5	7	39	6	20

Possible Conflicts matrix (Course Name/Number)

Course Name/Number	115	126	127	212	216	228	233	318	340	445	534	541	601	603	607
607 ADV. INSTR. MUSIC*	1	8	—	—	3	—	—	3	1	2	—	—	2	2	35
603 MUSIC THEORY*	—	—	—	—	—	—	2	—	—	—	—	2	4	6	—
601 INSTR. MUSIC*	4	—	1	4	—	8	3	—	—	—	2	2	48	4	—
541 OFF. PRAC.**	—	—	—	—	—	—	—	—	—	—	3	35	1	2	2
534 CLER. PRAC.*	—	—	—	—	—	—	—	—	—	—	15	3	3	—	2
445 PHYSICS**	18	—	—	15	1	15	—	1	5	35	—	—	8	—	—
340 FRENCH 9***	—	—	—	—	—	—	—	1	55	5	—	—	5	—	1
318 ITALIAN 12*	1	—	—	—	—	1	1	16	1	1	—	—	—	—	3
233 GEOMETRY***	—	—	—	—	—	—	60	1	—	—	—	3	2	—	—
228 ADV. MATH**	17	1	—	2	1	44	—	1	—	15	—	—	1	8	—
216 FUNCTIONS/RELATIONS*	—	—	—	1	14	1	—	—	—	1	—	—	—	—	3
212 CALCULUS*	15	—	—	18	2	—	—	—	—	15	—	—	4	—	—
127 ENGLISH 10B*	—	20	—	—	—	—	—	—	—	—	—	—	1	—	—
126 ENGLISH 10A*	18	—	—	—	1	—	—	—	—	—	—	—	—	8	—
115 CREATIVE WRITING*+	36	—	15	—	17	—	—	1	—	18	—	—	4	—	1

*Singleton
**Doubleton
***Tripleton

+Team taught
++Follows order recommended on page _____: singletons first, then doubletons, etc.

56

Period	1	2	3	4	5	6	7
Possible Conflicts		4				4	

To avoid conflicts, we must choose period 1, 3, 4, 5, or 6. We will opt for period 1 for several reasons: (1) students in all grades are enrolled in the course; (2) the room can be prepared prior to the start of school; and (3) the instructor has requested an early period. We list a "1" in the "Period Assigned" column. (See Figure 11.)

Figure 11

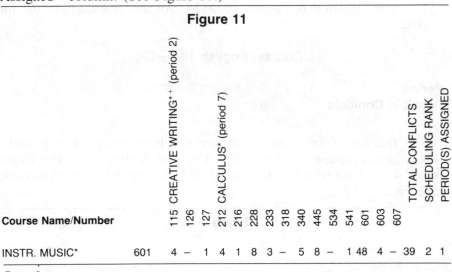

Course Name/Number		115 CREATIVE WRITING*+ (period 2)	126	127	212 CALCULUS* (period 7)	216	228	233	318	340	445	534	541	601	603	607	TOTAL CONFLICTS	SCHEDULING RANK	PERIOD(S) ASSIGNED
INSTR. MUSIC*	601	4	–	1	4	1	8	3	–	5	8	–	1	48	4	–	39	2	1

Step 6.

Since the third-ranked singleton, Calculus, is already scheduled (in period 7), we can move to Advanced Instrumental Music-607, following the same conflict analysis procedures.

Course: Advanced Instrumental Music—607

Period	1	2	3	4	5	6	7
Possible Conflicts		1					

Figure 12

Course Name/Number	115 CREAT.WRIT.*+ (period 2)	126	127	212	216	228	233	318	340	445	534	541	601	603	607	TOTAL CONFLICTS	SCHEDULING RANK	PERIOD(S) ASSIGNED
ADV. INSTR. MUSIC* 607	1	8	–	–	3	–	–	3	1	–	2	2	–	–	35	20	4	3

The only potential conflict is with Creative Writing-115 (period 2-one conflict). The matrix shows no conflict with either Calculus or Instrumental Music. But in our micro-schedule, there is only one music teacher. Period 1, then, is automatically a "teacher" conflict, since the instructor is already assigned to that period. (See Figure 11.) We can select any period except 1 or 2. We will choose period 3 for virtually the same reasons that placed Instrumental Music in period 1. (See Figure 12.)

Step 7.

The next singleton is English 10A-126. An analysis leads to the following:

Course: English 10A—126

Period	1	2	3	4	5	6	7
Possible Conflicts			8				

The teacher of this course has already been assigned to period 1 (Preparation/Planning), and period 2 (Creative Writing). We will choose period 4, since we wish to offer English 10A as early in the day as possible. (See Figure 13.)

Figure 13

Course Name/Number		115	126	127	212	216	228	233	318	340	445	534	541	601	603	607 ADV. INSTR. MUSIC* (period 3)	TOTAL CONFLICTS	SCHEDULING RANK	PERIOD(S) ASSIGNED
ENGLISH 10A*	126	–	18	–	–	–	–	–	1	–	–	–	–	–	–	–	8	9	5	4

Step 8.

We move next to Italian 12—318.

Course: Italian 12—318

Period	1	2	3	4	5	6	7
Possible Conflicts		1	3	1			

58

There are no special reasons for choosing either period 1, 5, 6, or 7 for this course. Not enough courses are scheduled for us to be concerned about ''balancing'' numbers of students assigned to each period. But an important principle of scheduling can enter the selection process at this point. This principle holds that *when non-conflicting singletons are identified in the matrix analysis, the scheduler should assign those singletons to the same period.* Italian 12 does not conflict with either Calculus (period 7) or Instrumental Music (period 1). We could, therefore, place it in either period 1 or period 7. Since there are many more students enrolled in Instrumental Music (48) than Calculus (18), we will assign Italian 12 to period 1. (See Figure 14.)

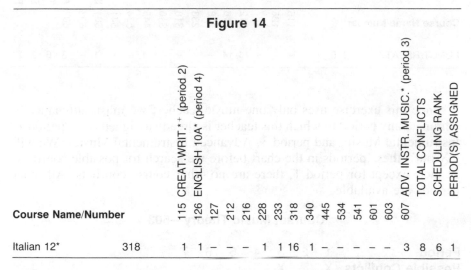

Figure 14

Course Name/Number		115 CREAT.WRIT.*+ (period 2)	126 ENGLISH 10A* (period 4)	127	212	216	228	233	318	340	445	534	541	601	603	607 ADV. INSTR. MUSIC.* (period 3)	TOTAL CONFLICTS	SCHEDULING RANK	PERIOD(S) ASSIGNED
Italian 12*	318	1	1	–	–	–	1	1	16	1	–	–	–	–	–	–	3	8	6 1

Step 9.

We apply this same methodology to the remaining singletons, remembering to follow the scheduling ranks established earlier.

Course: Functions/Relations—216

Period	1	2	3	4	5	6	7
Possible Conflicts	1		3				1

Functions/Relations has potential conflicts with Calculus (period 7-one conflict), Instrumental Music (period 1-one conflict), and Advanced Instrumental Music (period 3-three conflicts). Non-conflicting singletons already scheduled are Creative Writing (period 2), English 10A (period 4), and Italian 12 (period 1). Period 1 would produce a conflict with Instrumental Music. We will use period 2, since more students are enrolled in Creative Writing than English 10A or Italian 12. The value of this particular strategy will be evident if you project our micro-schedule into a real school schedule with many more courses than we are using here. Courses with higher enrollments tend to have greater potential for conflict than those with fewer students. (See Figure 15.)

59

Figure 15

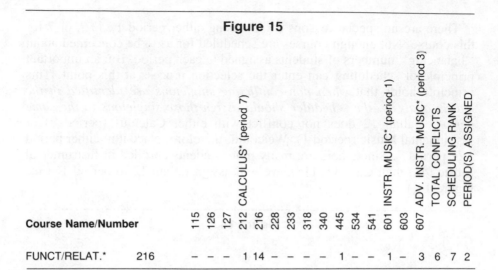

Course Name/Number		115	126	127	212 CALCULUS* (period 7)	216	228	233	318	340	445	534	541	601 INSTR. MUSIC* (period 1)	603	607 ADV. INSTR. MUSIC* (period 3)	TOTAL CONFLICTS	SCHEDULING RANK	PERIOD(S) ASSIGNED
FUNCT/RELAT.*	216	–	–	–	1	14	–	–	–	–	1	–	–	1	–	3	6	7	2

Step 10.

Since this exercise uses only one music teacher, we must automatically eliminate any period to which this teacher is already assigned (i.e., period 1, Instrumental Music, and period 3, Advanced Instrumental Music). We will "X-out" these periods in the chart before we search for possible conflicts. In fact, except for period 1, there are no other course conflicts. All other periods are available.

Course: Music Theory—603

Period	1	2	3	4	5	6	7
Possible Conflicts	X		X				

We might assign Music Theory to period 2 in light of our guideline about non-conflicting singletons (see Step 8), but this would give the music teacher three straight classes. Therefore, we will choose period 4. (See Figure 16.)

Figure 16

Course Name/Number		115	126	127	212	216	228	233	318	340	445	534	541	601 INSTR. MUSIC* (period 1)	603	607	TOTAL CONFLICTS	SCHEDULING RANK	PERIOD(S) ASSIGNED
MUSIC THEORY*	603	–	–	–	–	–	–	2	–	–	–	–	–	4	6	–	6	8	4

Step 11.

All periods but period 3 are available for Clerical Practices-534. Following our singleton guideline (Step 8), we will choose period 1. (See Figure 17.)

Course: Clerical Practices—534

Period	1	2	3	4	5	6	7
Possible Conflicts			2				

Figure 17

Course Name/Number		115	126	127	212	216	228	233	318	340	445	534	541	601	603	ADV. INSTR. MUSIC* (period 3) 607	TOTAL CONFLICTS	SCHEDULING RANK	PERIOD(S) ASSIGNED
CLER. PRAC.*	534	–	–	–	–	–	–	–	–	–	–	15	3	–	–	2	5	9	1

Step 12.

Every period but the first is suitable for English 10B. The English teacher, however, has already been assigned to periods 2 and 4. When we "X" these out, periods 3, 5, 6, or 7 remain. We will schedule English 10B in period 7 as a non-conflicting singleton. (See Figure 18.)

Course: English 10B—127

Period	1	2	3	4	5	6	7
Possible Conflicts	1	X		X			

Figure 18

Course Name/Number		115	126	127	212	216	228	233	318	340	445	534	541	INSTR. MUSIC* (period 1) 601	603	607	TOTAL CONFLICTS	SCHEDULING RANK	PERIOD(S) ASSIGNED
ENGLISH 10B*	127	–	–	20	–	–	–	–	–	–	–	–	–	1	–	–	1	10	7

We have now finished scheduling the singleton courses. By using our guidelines we have always been able to find one or more periods in the schedule where conflicts would not occur. If, however, as in a typical schedule, we had a large number of singletons, we would eventually have been forced to select periods that would produce the *fewest* number of conflicts. Consider the following example:

Course: Advanced Middle East History

Period	1	2	3	4	5	6	7
Possible Conflicts	12	15	8	35	42	19	22

Many conflicts exist in each period, but period 3 lists only eight. This period ordinarily would be the first choice, assuming that a subject teacher is available (not previously assigned). A second choice would be period 1 (12 conflicts), etc. A factor that might possibly affect the choice is room availability. Courses like stenography, clothing, woodworking, etc., are held in specialized rooms. Even if a particular period is the first choice because of fewer conflicts, its specialized room may already be scheduled during that period and thus preclude its use.

Doubletons

The next stage is the scheduling of doubletons. Since doubletons introduce new considerations, a brief review of "conflicts" to this point is warranted.

When the matrix signals a possible conflict between two singletons, one of two things is certain. If the scheduler places the singletons in the same period, a scheduling conflict will be created. The students affected will be unable to take one of the courses. On the other hand, if the two singletons are scheduled during different periods, no conflict will result and students can schedule both of them.

With doubletons, a variety of outcomes can occur.

If the matrix indicates a possible conflict between a doubleton and a singleton, no conflict will occur if each course is placed in a different period. If one of the doubleton sections is scheduled during the same period as the singleton *a conflict may or may not occur*. It is possible, though not always probable, that conflicting students may be scheduled into the other (non-conflicting) section. No scheduler ever knows this in advance.

Several possibilities exist when the matrix shows a possible conflict between two doubletons. If the two sections of each doubleton are scheduled independently of each other (i.e., not in the same period) there will be no conflicts. If one section of each pair is scheduled in the same period with the remaining sections in different periods *a conflict may or may not result*. Finally, the two sections of one doubleton may be placed in the same periods as the two sections of the other doubleton. Here the likelihood of a conflict is increased, although theoretically students can be "transferred" from one section to the other in each pair.

Different schedulers employ different strategies to deal with doubletons. We will utilize the "Least-Greatest" method for analyzing doubleton conflicts.

Whenever a singleton and doubleton are in potential conflict—whenever one section of the doubleton is offered at the same time as the singleton—we *assume* (a conservative convention) that *at least one-half* of the students will be in conflict (the *least* number, hypothetically). The most undesirable outcome, however, would be that all the students, the *greatest* number possible, would be in conflict. When completing our chart for each doubleton we enter the Least (L), and Greatest (G), number of possible conflicts. If the two courses, for example, showed 18 conflicts, the Least (L) figure would be 9, and the Greatest (G) 18.

Step 13.

For the first doubleton, Physics, only singleton-doubleton conflicts are possible. We must compute the "Least-Greatest" conflicts with Instrumental Music (period 1), Creative Writing and Functions/Relations (period 2), and Calculus (period 7). In period 2, for example, Creative Writing shows 18 conflicts for a "Least" of 9 and a "Greatest" of 18. Functions/Relations has only one conflict for an "L" of ½ and a "G" of 1. Total "L" is 9½; total "G" is 19.

Course: Physics—445

	1	2	3	4	5	6	7
	L G	L G	L G	L G	L G	L G	L G
Period							
Possible Conflicts	4 8	9 18					7½ 15
		½ 1					
		9½ 19					

The choices are periods 3, 4, 5, and 6. We will choose periods 3 and 4 for the two sections of Physics in our micro-schedule. This back-to-back arrangement allows the instructor to set up laboratory equipment for two consecutive classes. If Physics (or other science courses) required one or more additional lab periods for each section, we could select periods 3 and 5 for the regular classes, and schedule the lab or labs on alternate days in period 4. (See Figure 19.)

Step 14.

When both sections of a doubleton must be scheduled at the same time as those of a second doubleton, we can again assume that at *least* one-half of the students will be in conflict, and that the *greatest* number of possible conflicts will be the total number in the matrix. This technique is neither scientific nor absolute, so variations of it are employed by schedulers, also with great success. The principal advantage of the Least-Greatest approach is that it is conservative and therefore highly successful.

Figure 19

Course Name/Number	115	126	127	212	216	228	233	318	340	445	534	541	601	603	607
PERIOD(S) ASSIGNED	2	4	7	7	2					1			3,4	1	3
SCHEDULING RANK++	1	5	10	3	7	2	12	15	6	14	11	9	13	8	4
TOTAL CONFLICTS	56	9	—	37	6	44	6	8	7	57	5	7	39	6	20
115 CREATIVE WRITING*+	36	—	—	15	—	17	—	1	—	18	—	—	4	—	1
126 ENGLISH 10A*	—	18	—	—	—	—	—	—	—	—	—	—	—	—	8
127 ENGLISH 10B*	—	—	20	—	—	—	—	—	—	—	—	—	—	—	—
212 CALCULUS*	15	—	—	18	1	2	—	—	—	15	—	—	4	—	—
216 FUNCTIONS/RELATIONS*	—	—	—	1	14	1	—	—	—	—	—	—	—	—	3
228 ADV. MATH**	17	—	—	2	1	44	—	—	—	15	—	—	8	—	1
233 GEOMETRY***	—	—	—	—	—	—	60	1	—	—	3	—	2	—	—
318 ITALIAN 12*	1	—	—	—	—	—	1	16	1	1	—	—	—	—	3
340 FRENCH 9***	—	—	—	—	—	—	—	1	55	—	—	—	5	—	1
445 PHYSICS**	18	—	—	15	—	15	—	1	—	35	—	—	8	—	—
534 CLER. PRAC.*	—	—	—	—	—	—	3	—	—	—	15	3	—	—	—
541 OFF. PRAC.**	—	—	—	—	—	—	—	—	—	—	3	35	1	—	—
601 INSTR. MUSIC*	4	—	—	4	—	8	2	—	5	8	—	1	48	4	3
603 MUSIC THEORY*	—	—	—	—	—	—	—	—	—	—	—	—	4	6	—
607 ADV. INSTR. MUSIC*	1	8	—	—	3	1	—	3	1	—	—	—	3	—	35

*Singleton
**Doubleton
***Tripleton

+Team taught
++Follows order recommended on page _____ : singletons first, then doubletons, etc.

Let us apply the strategy to Advanced Math-228. (See Figure 19 for the entire matrix.) Conflicts existing with Advanced Math-228 include: Italian 12 and Instrumental Music (period 1), Creative Writing (period 2), Physics (periods 3 and 4), and Calculus (period 7). In period 1, for example, Italian 12 with one conflict and Instrumental Music with 8 conflicts result in an "L" of ½ + 4 and a "G" of 1 + 8.

Course: Advanced Math—228

Period	1		2		3		4		5		6		7	
	L	G	L	G	L	G	L	G	L	G	L	G	L	G
Possible Conflicts	½	1	8½	19	7½	15	7½	15					1	2
	4	8												
	4½	9												

Since no conflicts emerge in either periods 5 or 6, we select them. If consecutive periods were inadvisable in some circumstances, then period 7 with 2 conflicts would be workable (fewest conflicts). Note that the only doubleton-doubleton conflict is with Physics, which we scheduled in periods 3 and 4. (See Figure 20.)

Figure 20

Course Name/Number	115 CREAT. WRIT.* (period 2)	126	127	212 CALCULUS* (period 7)	216	228	233	318 ITALIAN 12* (period 1)	340	445 PHYSICS** (periods 3, 4)	534	541	601 INSTR. MUSIC* (period 1)	603	607	TOTAL CONFLICTS	SCHEDULING RANK	PERIOD(S) ASSIGNED
ADV. MATH** 228	17	–	–	2	–	44	–	1	–	15	–	1	8	–	–	44	12	5,6

Step 15.

The final doubleton is Office Practices-541. Conflicts exist with Clerical Practices and Instrumental Music (period 1), Advanced Instrumental Music (period 3), and Advanced Math (periods 5 and 6).

Course: Office Practices—541

Period	1		2		3		4		5		6		7	
	L	G	L	G	L	G	L	G	L	G	L	G	L	G
Possible Conflicts	1½	3			1	2			½	1	½	1		
	½	1												
	2	4												

Periods 2, 4, and 7 are free of any possible conflicts. We will use periods 2 and 4 to offer this course in the morning. Many of the enrolled students leave school after period 5 for work experience in the community. (See Figure 21.)

Figure 21

Course Name/Number		115	126	127	212	216	228 ADV. MATH** (periods 5, 6)	233	318	340	445	534 CLER. PRAC.* (period 1)	541 INSTR. MUSIC* (period 1)	601 INSTR. MUSIC* (period 1)	603	607 ADV. INSTR. MUSIC.* (period 3)	TOTAL CONFLICTS	SCHEDULING RANK	PERIOD(S) ASSIGNED
OFF. PRAC.**	541	–	–	–	–	–	1	–	–	–	–	3	35	1	–	2	7	13	2,4

Tripletons

Step 16.

The two remaining courses are tripletons. Again, we will take a conservative posture by computing the *Least* and *Greatest* number of potential conflicts. For singleton-tripleton conflicts, we will assume the *least* number of conflicts will be one-third of the figure in the matrix, and the *greatest,* two-thirds. For the doubleton-tripleton combinations, the *least* will be one-half, and the *greatest,* two-thirds. And for the tripleton-tripleton conflicts, the *least* will be two-thirds, and the *greatest,* the total number.

Consider the first tripleton: French 9-340. Conflicts exist with Italian 12 and Instrumental Music (period 1), and Advanced Instrumental Music (period 3).

Course: French 9—340

	1		2		3		4		5		6		7	
Period	L	G	L	G	L	G	L	G	L	G	L	G	L	G
Possible Conflicts	⅓	⅔			⅓	⅔								

$$\frac{1⅔ \quad 3⅓}{2 \quad \ \ 4}$$

The scheduler has a wide choice of periods. Since periods 5 and 6 have been selected only once, we will use them along with period 2 to highlight the need to balance students throughout all seven periods. (See Figure 22.)

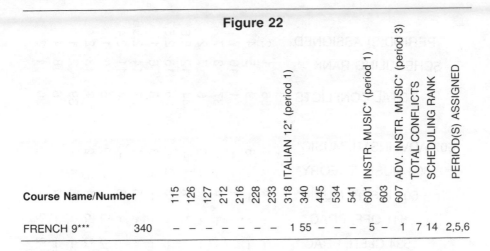

Figure 22

Course Name/Number		115	126	127	212	216	228	233	318 ITALIAN 12* (period 1)	340	445	534	541	601 INSTR. MUSIC* (period 1)	603	607 ADV. INSTR. MUSIC* (period 3)	TOTAL CONFLICTS	SCHEDULING RANK	PERIOD(S) ASSIGNED
FRENCH 9***	340	–	–	–	–	–	–	–	1	55	–	–	–	5	–	1	7	14	2,5,6

Step 17.

The last tripleton and final course in our micro-schedule is Geometry-233. Conflicts are with Italian 12 and Instrumental Music (period 1), and Music Theory (period 4).

Course: Geometry—233

	1		2		3		4		5		6		7	
Period	L	G	L	G	L	G	L	G	L	G	L	G	L	G
Possible Conflicts	⅓	⅔					⅔	1⅓						
	1	2												
	1⅓	2⅔												

Again we have several alternatives. Checking the assignments of the two math teachers (see Figures 24 and 25), we note that math teacher A is previously assigned to periods 2 and 5 (or 6); math teacher B to periods 6 (or 5) and 7. We can place one or more sections of Geometry in periods 5, 6, or 7, as long as we balance these teachers with sections of Advanced Mathematics. We will assign two sections of Geometry to periods 2 and 5 with math teacher B, and the third section to period 7 with math teacher A. (See Figure 23.)

After the tripletons have been assigned in an actual schedule, the scheduler continues with the four-section courses, five-section courses, etc. Great attention must be paid at this stage to balancing the number of students in each period. A printing calculator is a necessity for this operation.

Building the Master Schedule

When all sections of all courses have been assigned to specific periods, the scheduler should prepare a teacher assignment chart similar to the one in Figure 24. The material in this chart was part of our available documentation for the micro-schedule. When teacher assignments are completed, the information should be transferred to the Master Schedule (Figure 25). This

Figure 23

Course Name/Number	115	126	127	212	216	228	233	318	340	445	534	541	601	603	607
PERIOD(S) ASSIGNED	2	4	7	7	2	5,6	2,5,7	1	2,5,6	3,4	1	2,4	1	4	3
SCHEDULING RANK++	1	5	10	3	7	12	15	6	14	11	9	13	2	8	4
TOTAL CONFLICTS	56	9	1	37	6	44	6	8	7	57	5	7	39	6	20
607 ADV. INSTR. MUSIC*	1	8	—	—	3	—	3	1	—	—	2	2	—	—	35
603 MUSIC THEORY*	1	—	—	—	—	1	—	—	—	—	—	—	4	6	—
601 INSTR. MUSIC*	4	1	1	4	—	8	3	—	5	8	—	1	48	4	—
541 OFF. PRAC.**	—	—	—	—	—	—	—	3	—	—	1	35	1	—	2
534 CLER. PRAC.*	—	—	—	—	—	—	—	2	—	—	15	1	—	—	2
445 PHYSICS**	18	—	—	15	1	15	—	—	—	35	—	—	8	—	—
340 FRENCH 9***	—	—	—	—	—	—	—	2	55	—	—	—	5	—	—
318 ITALIAN 12*	—	—	—	—	—	—	—	16	2	—	2	3	—	—	1
233 GEOMETRY***	—	—	—	—	—	—	60	—	—	—	—	—	3	—	3
228 ADV. MATH**	17	—	—	2	1	44	—	—	—	15	—	—	8	1	—
216 FUNCTIONS/RELATIONS*	—	—	—	1	14	1	—	—	—	1	—	—	—	—	3
212 CALCULUS*	15	—	—	18	1	2	—	—	—	15	—	—	4	—	—
127 ENGLISH 10B*	—	—	20	—	—	—	—	—	—	—	—	—	1	—	—
126 ENGLISH 10A*	—	18	—	—	—	—	—	—	—	—	—	—	1	—	8
115 CREATIVE WRITING*+	36	—	—	15	—	17	—	—	—	18	—	—	4	1	1

+ Team taught
++ Follows order recommended on page _____ : singletons first, then doubletons, etc.

*Singleton
**Doubleton
***Tripleton

68

same procedure would be utilized in the construction of an actual school schedule, but a large scheduling chart or book would be necessary to list all the courses and teachers.

Note in Figure 25 that the left-hand column is arranged by department. Teachers are listed in alphabetical order within each department. The seven periods are displayed across the top of the chart. (Teachers and periods may be reversed if that is more convenient.) Under period 1, for example, Clerical Practices is listed opposite business teacher B. The "15" in the small box represents the number of students enrolled in the course. Listing room numbers for each section is also advisable (although not shown here) to preclude the inadvertent assignment of two or more classes to the same room in the same period. When entering a doubleton such as Physics, we place one-half the number of students in one box (rounded up for uneven numbers) and one-half in the other. Science teacher A in periods 3 and 4 illustrates this procedure.

Figure 24

Teacher Assignment Chart by Department

ENGLISH TEACHER A	1—English 10A; 1—English 10B; 1—Creative Writing
ENGLISH TEACHER B	1—Creative Writing
MATH TEACHER A	1—Functions/Relations; 1—Advanced Math; 1—Geometry
MATH TEACHER B	1—Calculus; 2—Geometry; 1—Advanced Math
SCIENCE TEACHER A	2—Physics
MOD. LANG. TEACHER A	2—French 9; 1—Italian 12
BUSINESS TEACHER A	2—Office Practices
BUSINESS TEACHER B	1—Clerical Practices
MUSIC TEACHER A	1—Music Theory; 1—Instrumental Music; 1—Advanced Instrumental Music

---

Scheduling Aids

Many schools use large chalkboards or magnetic boards to lay out the master schedule. Some type of visualization device is very important, because the amount of information summarized in the master schedule can be monumental. It is very easy to forget someone or something—and excessive conflicts can be the result.

Several kinds of commercial scheduling boards are available (at high cost), but a school administrator can easily make a personal scheduling book to lay out departmental (or team) schedules.[1] The book consists of an

---

1. The "Scheduling Book" concept was developed in 1963 at Pius X High School, Downey, Calif. by James W. Keefe, now NASSP director of research.

ordinary loose leaf notebook and separate loose leaf pages made from stamp collector's stock pages (8 to 12 pockets, depending on the number of school periods or modules). These stock pages can be purchased from a stamp supply dealer or ordered from a vinyl supply house.

The scheduler should line the stock pages for the number of required periods/mods, as illustrated in Figures 26 and 27. Teacher names and class offerings should be written on one-inch square card or paper tabs so that they can be moved around on the page as desired.

Photocopies can easily be made of the intermediate or final schedules—either for reference, or as a basis for the composite, school-wide schedule. The entire book is portable and secure, unlike scheduling boards that must be mounted on a wall.

Ultimately, very sophisticated teacher schedules can be derived from the basic master schedule. Figure 28 shows an individualized two-week schedule for an English teacher at Bishop Carroll High School, Calgary, Alberta.

Figure 25
Master Schedule Chart

Department/Teacher	1	2	3	4	5	6	7
English Teacher A	Planning and Prep.	Creat. Writ. 18		Eng. 10A 18			Eng. 10B 20
English Teacher B	Planning and Prep.	Creat. Writ. 18					
Math Teacher A		Funct./Relat. 14			Adv. Math 22		Geom. 20
Math Teacher B		Geom. 20			Geom. 20	Adv. Math 22	Calculus 18
Science Teacher A			Physics 18	Physics 17			
For. Lang. Teacher A	Italian 12 16	French 9 19			French 9 18	French 9 18	
Business Teacher A		Off. Pract. 18		Off. Pract. 17			
Business Teacher B	Cler. Prac. 15						
Music Teacher A	Instr. Music 48		Adv. Instr. Music 35	Music Theory 6			

71

Figure 26
Scheduling Book (Periods)

PERIOD TEACHER	1	2	3	4	5	6	7
BOND	ENG 1	ENG 1	PREP				
CLARKE			PREP	ENG 2	ENG 2		
JONES			WRITING LAB		LUNCH		
LAMPE		JOURNAL.	JOURNAL.	JOURNAL.			
RYAN					PREP	ENG 3	ENG 3
SMITH	ADV. PLACE. ENG	ADV. PLACE. ENG		LUNCH	OFFICE		
ZALE					ENG 4	ENG 4	ENG 4

Figure 27
Scheduling Book (Mods)

MOD	BOND	CLARKE	JONES	LAMPE	RYAN	SMITH	ZALE
C O U R S E S (BY TEACHER NAME)							
1	ENG 1						
2	ENG 1						
3				JOURNALISM			
4	PREP.	PREP.	WRIT. LAB	JOURNALISM		ADV. PLACE.	
5		ENG 2		JOURNALISM		ADV. PLACE.	
6		ENG 2					
7			LUNCH		PREP.	OFFICE	
8					ENG 3	LUNCH	
9					ENG 3		ENG 4
10							ENG 4
11							ENG 4
12							

Figure 28
Teacher Schedule (Individualized)

T-A Jones, Robert   SUBJECT AREA   ENGLISH

	WEEK A					WEEK B				
	MON.	TUES.	WED.	THURS.	FRI.	MON.	TUES.	WED.	THURS.	FRI.
L.G.P.	Practical Arts	H.F.R.	Social Science	English L.A.	Religious Studies	Modern Language		Fine Arts	Math	Science
8:50	T-A STUDENT CHECK-IN					T-A STUDENT CHECK-IN				
9:00	Resource Center	T-A	Resource Center	Seminar	Resource Center	T-A	Curr. Work	Resource Center	Seminar	Resource Center
10:00	Resource Center	T-A	Curr. Work	T-A	Resource Center	Resource Center	Curr. Work	Resource Center	Marking	Resource Center
11:00	Resource Center	T-A	Curr. Work	T-A / LUNCH	Resource Center	Resource Center	Curr. Work	Resource Center	Marking / LUNCH	Resource Center
12:00	LUNCH / Marking	LUNCH		Resource Center	LUNCH	LUNCH	LUNCH	LUNCH	Resource Center	LUNCH
1:00	Seminar	Marking		Resource Center	Seminar Comm.	Seminar	T-A	T-A	Resource Center	Cinema Carroll
2:00	Seminar	Resource Center		Resource Center	Marking	Seminar	Resource Center	Marking	Resource Center	T-A
2:50	T-A STUDENT CHECK-OUT					T-A STUDENT CHECK-OUT				
AREA CLOSED	H.F.R.	Social Science	English	Religious Studies	Modern Language	Fine Arts		Math	Science	Practical Arts

74

Chapter Six
Summary and Suggestions

THE SCHEDULING PROCESS is embedded in every strand of a school's organizational fabric. The principal must establish direction for the scheduling
process, ensuring correspondence among objectives, format, method-
ologies, and the philosophical foundations of the school.

A secondary school cannot function without competent scheduling. The
curriculum is activated through scheduling; students proceed through the
program of studies as a result of scheduling; teachers are assigned to students through scheduling. In short, scheduling sets the stage for learning.

Both new and experienced principals can bring a valuable perspective to
the scheduling process. Newly appointed principals bring a fresh viewpoint.
They ask such questions as "Why?" or, "Is there a better way?" Veteran
administrators can compare their scheduling models and procedures with
those of other colleagues and with examples from the literature. In either
case, the principal must seek ways to use the schedule to better achieve the
goals and objectives of the school.

Scheduling has a number of phases which must occur whether manual or
computerized techniques are employed. The major phases are:

1.	Prescheduling (preparing)	Manual
2.	Registration (collecting data)	Manual or Computer
3.	Building the master schedule	Manual or Computer
4.	Scheduling students (loading)	Manual or Computer

The most consequential of these phases is prescheduling, when procedures are developed to ensure congruence between goals, curriculum, and
strategies formulated to collect the data from which teacher and student
schedules are generated. Prescheduling involves decisions about a variety of
topics. Among the most important are determination of local and state
curricular mandates, length of courses, periods in the school day, days in the
scheduling cycle, use of school-within-school plans, and modifications of
conventional programs. Each of these areas must be assessed periodically to
determine whether existing patterns should be changed.

The principal must analyze staffing patterns very carefully in times of
declining enrollment. Fewer students mean fewer sections of courses, the

consolidation of elective offerings, and possible need for dual certification of many teachers. Proper use of enrollment projections can lessen the adverse effect of diminishing numbers.

The prescheduling process assumes thorough familiarity with the program of studies and the building itself. The curriculum, its required and elective courses, and its promotion and graduation requirements must be fully understood. The registration procedure must open lines of communication among students, teachers, counselors, administrators, and parents. Knowledgeable schedulers are sensitive to all restrictive factors that may reduce flexibility in the scheduling cycle, particularly those arising from unusual building characteristics, particular courses, or the terms of the negotiated contract.

The selection of a scheduling model must be based upon what is best for student learning. No place exists for fads in scheduling. The choice of a schedule should flow from the philosophy of the school and community. Conventional schedules are appropriate in some schools and districts, while flexible modular and even individualized varieties are suitable in others. There is no ideal schedule. Decisions must also be made about the procedures to be used in scheduling (manual or computerized), the degree of student participation (standard or student self-scheduling), and a realistic calendar for the scheduling cycle.

In the registration phases, course tallies must be interpreted to identify staffing needs and to determine final course offerings. A conflict matrix can be produced either by machine or by hand. The matrix then is used to build an efficient master schedule. Building the master schedule assumes the availability of the following information and/or materials:

- Times for opening and closing of school;
- Length of courses and class periods;
- Days in the scheduling cycle;
- Time for lunch periods, passing periods, etc.;
- Class size limits and the minimum/maximum number of students needed to offer each course;
- Number, size, and special facilities of classrooms;
- Number of teachers available (or number to be employed) and their teaching preferences;
- Course offerings and organization of the curriculum;
- Bases for any special grouping and assignment to special classes;
- Organization of any special schedules (assembly period, early release, laboratory or shop periods, overlapping sessions, extended school year programs, etc.);
- Student selection of courses (preregistration);
- A scheduling board, scheduling book, key sort cards, or computerized scheduling forms;
- Printout of master schedule and student programs.

The scheduling process can consume the greater part of several months and its successful completion is a prime responsibility of the principal. Yet in virtually all respects, efficient scheduling is a prime contributor to the overall success of the school year.

76

The opening days of the school year frequently reflect the amount of attention given to the development of the master schedule and the appropriateness of the strategies devised to implement it. Student schedule changes are a good barometer of this attention and efficiency: Many schools have evolved clearly-articulated policies balancing firmness and fairness to accommodate legitimate student course change requests and to obviate frivolous ones.

Student requests for course changes are usually characterized by one or more of the following conditions:

1. *Scheduling errors.* Some students receive schedule cards with obvious errors. They should be directed to visit the appropriate guidance or administrative office to have correct assignments made.

2. *Program changes.* At various stages of their high school career, certain students (and/or their parents) realize that a change in their basic school program is warranted; e.g., a switch from the college preparatory curriculum to a vocationally-oriented one, or vice versa. Although such changes should be initiated during the summer months, many students defer contacting the school until the start of the new year. Obviously, these students should be seen as soon as possible and provided with appropriate counseling assistance.

3. *Significant course changes.* Some students, while not requiring a total change in program, may wish to alter certain courses based on their (demonstrated) inability to pursue a particular curricular sequence (e.g., math). Other students need to be separated from teachers with whom they were unsuccessful in the past. These changes should be processed within the first few days of school.

4. *Frivolous course changes.* The folly of individual requests for program change is a matter of viewpoint, but reducing requests to a minimum appears to be a worthy goal. One effective strategy is to authorize only the above three types of changes during the opening weeks of school. The resulting delay may discourage some students from pursuing frivolous requests. Establishing a chain of required approvals, including counselors, the director of guidance, a vice principal, and/or even the principal will usually deter others from the attempt.

A wide variety of articles on scheduling will be found in the accompanying bibliography. The literature can be helpful in guiding administrators toward scheduling practices that enhance student learning. Another useful step before implementing any schedule change is to visit a number of schools that are using the particular scheduling program. The more fully the principal, the scheduler, and the staff members are informed, especially from firsthand experience, the better will the scheduling process reflect and implement the school program.

Glossary of Terms

Arena—The name given to the physical site where student self-scheduling (arena scheduling) takes place. Often, it is the school gymnasium or other large multi-use area.

Arena Scheduling—An optional stage of the load phase of scheduling in which students generate their own individual schedules. Often called self-scheduling.

Block Scheduling—Placement of students with common subject selections into larger class groupings, often scheduled for longer blocks of time throughout the day.

Build Phase—An intermediate phase of the scheduling process consisting of the conflict matrix and schedule-building steps that ultimately result in the construction of the master schedule. Also called the "generation" phase.

Common Core Schedule—A schedule that combines groups of students into units of similar courses for which they have enrolled, or which the school or school district deems necessary.

Computer Scheduling—A general term describing the use of a computer to assist in student scheduling. The range of such assistance extends from the preparation of simple reports or printouts to the complete processing of both the master schedule and individual student schedules.

Conflict—Conflict is a condition in which two or more courses selected by a student are offered at the same time. A student is forced to delete one selection and replace it with another allowable by the master schedule.

Conflict Matrix—A square display of all courses that outlines the number of students who have signed up for each pair of courses offered in the curriculum.

Conventional Schedule—A traditional scheduling method based on a weekly cycle of class periods of equal length, usually meeting at the same time each day. Most conventional schedules have six to eight periods.

Course Tallies—Enrollment figures for each course offered in the curriculum.

Course Verification Report—A report produced by the computer (along with course tallies), intended for dissemination to parents, which lists those courses for which their students have enrolled.

Daily Demand Schedule—A highly individualized and flexible schedule which changes every day based on the recommendations of subject area (departmental) teams.

Days-in-Cycle—The number of days from the beginning of a schedule pattern to its conclusion. When the pattern repeats, a new cycle has begun. Most schools operate on a five-day cycle, Monday through Friday.

Double Block—The scheduling of a subject for two consecutive periods.

Doubleton—A course which has sufficient enrollment to require two separate and distinct sections.

Flexible Modular Schedule—A type of schedule that divides the school day into 15 to 30 abbreviated periods (10 to 20 minutes each) in order to provide a greater variety of instructional experiences such as large-group, small-group, and independent study.

Fluid Block Schedule—A block schedule which assigns a group of students to a team of teachers for large segments of instructional time in predetermined subject areas.

Generation Phase—Synonym for *Build Phase*.

House Plan—An organizational plan that divides a larger school into smaller administrative units called "houses" or "schools-within-a-school." Each house may have its own administrator, faculty, classrooms, program of studies, and unique scheduling process. House plans may include a conventional school-within-a-school, a flexible modular program, a career unit, etc.

Individualized Scheduling—Highly personalized scheduling arrangements built on variable time credit or continuous progress sequences, with greater opportunity for student self-scheduling, more time for individual projects, and fewer whole-class activities.

Load Phase—The final phase of scheduling, wherein student course requests are merged with the master schedule to produce student schedules and class lists.

Manual Scheduling—The completion of the scheduling process by hand, without computerized data processing assistance.

Master Schedule—A comprehensive listing of the program of studies that assigns every section of every course to specific teachers in designated rooms at various times of the day.

Mosaic Scheduling—a loading technique used to schedule student courses (usually electives) individually rather than in block (group) fashion.

Partial Block Pattern—A modification of block scheduling in which student electives are scheduled with the mosaic method after required courses have been enrolled using the block method.

Period Flexible Schedule—A slightly modified traditional schedule in which the lengths of periods vary throughout the cycle.

Pontoon Transitional Schedule—A block schedule that interrelates two or more subjects in a flexible block of time using large-group and small-group instruction, team teaching, and individual study.

Rotating (Period) Schedule—A conventional or flexible modular schedule in which the periods are rotated each day so that subjects fall in different time frames of the cycle.

Scheduling—The process by which the curriculum, the students, and the teachers are brought together in an organized manner.

Scheduling Cycle—The series of interrelated steps starting with the identification of student curricular needs and ending with the distribution of schedules to students. The cycle is made visible in the scheduling calendar.

School-Within-a-School—See *House Plan.*

Simulation Run—A computerized testing of the efficiency of the master schedule in which problems and possible solutions are identified.

Single-Double Exchange Schedule—A schedule which allows each subject to meet five periods during a five-day cycle, one day for two consecutive periods, and not at all another day.

Singleton—A course which has only one section, regardless of the enrollment. A common example is band or chorus.

Standard Scheduling—Administrative (office) assignment of students to classes during the load phase of scheduling.

Static Schedule—A conventional or flexible modular schedule in which the subjects meet at the same time each day of the cycle.

Student Self-Scheduling—A synonym for *Arena Scheduling.*

Total Cycle Interchange—A rearrangement of the periods in the school day so that no section of a course meets at the same time throughout the cycle.

Traditional Schedule—A synonym for a *Conventional Schedule.*

Tripleton—A course that has sufficient enrollment to require three separate and distinct sections.

SELECTED REFERENCES

Alexander, William M.; Saylor, J. Galen; and Williams, Emmett L. *The High School—Today and Tomorrow*. New York: Holt, Rinehart, & Winston, 1971.

Alexander, William M.; Williams, Emmett L.; Compton, Mary; Hines, Vynce A.; and Prescott, Dan. *The Emergent Middle School*. New York: Holt, Rinehart, & Winston, 1968.

Anderson, Lester W., and Van Dyke, Lauren A. *Secondary School Administration*. 2d ed. Boston: Houghton Mifflin Co., 1972.

Austin, David B., and Gividen, Nobel. *The High School Principal and Staff Develop the Master Schedule*. New York: Columbia University Press, 1960.

Barker, Brian H.; Penningroth, Gerald; and Rogers, John F. "Arena vs. Computer Scheduling." *NASSP Bulletin*, March 1980, pp. 114-16.

Beggs, David W., III. *Team Teaching—Bold New Venture*. Bloomington: Indiana University Press, 1964.

Beggs, David W., III, and Manlove, Donald C. *Flexible Scheduling Using the Indi-Flex S Model*. Bloomington: Indiana University Press, 1965.

Bossing, Nelson, and Cramer, Roscoe V. *The Junior High School*. Boston: Houghton Mifflin Co., 1965.

Boylan, Eugene T. "Block Program Helps Teachers Plan Individualized Instruction." *NASSP Bulletin*, May 1980, pp. 111-12.

Brown, F. Frank. *New Directions for the Comprehensive High School*. West Nyack, N.Y.: Parker Publishing Co., 1972.

Bush, Robert N., and Allen, Dwight W. *A New Design for High School Education*. New York: McGraw-Hill, 1964.

Bushnell, Don D., and Allen, Dwight W. *The Computer in American Education*. New York: Wiley, 1967.

Clark, Leonard H. "Teaching Load Formulas Compared." *NASSP Bulletin*, October 1956, pp. 55-62.

DeLucia, Joseph J. "R.E.O.—A Flexible Modular Schedule with Accountability." *NASSP Bulletin*, September 1977, pp. 115-17.

Dougherty, John W., and Perkins, William. "Scheduling Problems Caused by Declining Enrollments." *NASSP Bulletin*, May 1980, pp. 110-11.

Douglass, Harl R. *Modern Administration of Secondary Schools*. 2d ed. New York: Blaisdell Publishing Co., 1963.

"Five Flexible Schedules That Work." *Nation's Schools*, August 1968, pp. 28-31.

Georgiades, William; Keefe, James W.; Lowery, Robert E.; Anderson, Wesley R.; McLean, A. F.; Milliken, Robert; Udinsky, B. Flavian; and Warner, Wayne. *Take Five: A Methodology for the Humane School*. Los Angeles: Parker & Son, 1979.

Glatthorn, Allan A. *Alternatives in Education: Schools and Programs*. New York: Dodd, Mead & Co., 1975.

Gruhn, William T., and Douglass, Harl R. *The Modern Junior High School*. New York: The Ronald Press, 1971.

Heller, Robert W.; Chaffee, Leonard M.; and Davison, Ronald G. "Two Computer-Based School Scheduling Programs Analyzed." *NASSP Bulletin*, March 1974, pp. 64-82.

Herriott, M. E. "The Master Schedule of Classes in Junior High School." *California Journal of Secondary Education*, November 1959, pp. 403-7.

Hughes, Larry W., and Ubben, Gerald C. *The Secondary Principal's Handbook: A Guide to Executive Action*. Boston: Allyn and Bacon, 1980.

Jacobson, Paul B.; Reaves, William C.; and Logsdon, James D. *The Effective School Principal*. 2d ed. Englewood Cliffs, N.J.: Prentice-Hall, 1963.

Johnson, Howard M. "Flexibility in the Secondary School." *NASSP Bulletin,* October 1969, pp. 62-72.

Johnson, Robert H., and Lobb, M. Delbert. "The Transformation of the Sacred Secondary-School Schedule." *California Journal of Secondary Education,* February 1960, pp. 96-105.

Keefe, James W. "Pius X High School." *NASSP Bulletin,* November 1977, pp. 85-95.

Kelly, Larry K. "Student Self-Scheduling—Is It Worth the Risk?" *NASSP Bulletin,* February 1979, pp. 84-91.

Kenney, James B., and Rentz, R. Robert. *Automation and Control of Public School Instructional Records.* Itasca, Ill.: F. E. Peacock, 1970.

Kohut, Sylvester, Jr. *The Middle School: A Bridge Between Elementary and Secondary Schools.* Washington, D.C.: National Education Association, 1976.

Landers, Thomas J., and Myers, Judith G. *Essentials of School Management.* Philadelphia, Pa.: W. B. Saunders, 1977.

Levanto, Joseph. "Mr. Computer—Assistant Principal." *Journal of Secondary Education,* March 1968, pp. 113-23.

Lowery, Robert E. "Bishop Carroll High School." *NASSP Bulletin,* November 1977, pp. 10-20.

Mack, A. Russell. "The 'Rotating' Schedule." *NASSP Bulletin,* November 1947, pp. 25-30.

Murphy, Judith. *School Scheduling by Computer: The Story of GASP.* New York: Educational Facilities Laboratory, 1964.

Parker, Jack. "Intangibles in the Master Schedule." *NASSP Bulletin,* October 1974, pp. 79-83.

Petroquin, Gaynor. *Individualizing Learning Through Modular-Flexible Programming.* New York: McGraw-Hill, 1968.

Saville, Anthony. *Instructional Programming: Issues and Innovations in School Scheduling.* Columbus, Ohio: Charles E. Merrill, 1973.

Scala, Anthony W. "Year-Round School." *NASSP Bulletin,* March 1970, pp. 79-89.

Shaten, N. Lewis. "Building the Schedule: Breaking from the Mold of Traditional Thinking." *NASSP Bulletin,* February 1982, pp. 91-95.

Shockloss, Daniel P. "Changing to Modular Flexible Scheduling." *NASSP Bulletin,* January 1973, pp. 79-88.

Swaab, Alexander M. *School Administrator's Guide to Flexible Modular Scheduling.* West Nyack, N.Y.: Parker Publishing Co., 1974.

Traverso, Henry P. "The Six-Day Cycle—A Viable Scheduling Option." *NASSP Bulletin,* December 1980, pp. 87-91.

Trump, J. Lloyd, and Georgiades, William. "Doing Better with What You Have— NASSP Model Schools Project." *NASSP Bulletin,* May 1970, pp. 106-33.

Trump, J. Lloyd, and Miller, Delmas F. *Secondary School Curriculum Improvement: Challenges, Humanism, Accountability.* 2d ed. Boston: Allyn and Bacon, 1973.

Ubben, Gerald C. "A Fluid Block Schedule." *NASSP Bulletin,* February 1976, pp. 104-11.

Wall, F. Edward. "Class Schedules—Computer Loaded or Student Self-Scheduled?" *NASSP Bulletin,* May 1979, pp. 93-97.

Wall, F. Edward. "Student Self-Scheduling Works Well for Us." *NASSP Bulletin,* February 1976, pp. 99-103.

Wiley, Deane, and Bishop, Lloyd. *The Flexibly Scheduled High School*. West Nyack, N.Y.: Parker Publishing Co., 1961.

Williams, Stirling B., Jr., and Siler, Larry E. "Mini-Computers Can Work for Registration and Scheduling." *NASSP Bulletin,* December 1980, pp. 109-13.

Wood, Charles L. "Modular Scheduling? Yes, But—." *Journal of Secondary Education,* January 1970, pp. 40-42.

About the authors:

Richard A. Dempsey is professor and chairman of the department of curriculum and instruction at the University of Connecticut. He is a former member of the NASSP Committee of Professors of Secondary School Administration and Supervision.

Henry P. Traverso is director of curriculum for Regional School District 10, Burlington-Harwinton, Conn., and a former high school principal.